McGraw-Hill's
Proofreading
Handbook

SECOND EDITION

#

Laura ⌐Anderson

McGraw·Hill

New York   Chicago   San Francisco   Lisbon   London   Madrid   Mexico City
Milan   New Delhi   San Juan   Seoul   Singapore   Sydney   Toronto

The *McGraw-Hill* Companies

Library of Congress Cataloging-in-Publication Data

Anderson, Laura Killen, 1938–
    McGraw-Hill's proofreading handbook / Laura Anderson.—2nd ed.
      p. cm.
    Rev. ed. of: Handbook for proofreading. c1990.
    ISBN 0-07-145764-X (acid-free paper)

    1. Proofreading—Handbooks, manuals, etc. I. Title: Proofreading
handbook. II. Anderson, Laura Killen, 1938– Handbook for proofreading.
III. Title.

Z254.A5 2005
686.2'255—dc22   *686.2255*   2005047977

1 2 3 4 5 6 7 8 9 0   FGR/FGR   0 9 8 7 6 5

ISBN 0-07-145764-X

McGraw-Hill books are available at special quantity discounts to use as
premiums and sales promotions, or for use in corporate training programs.
For more information, please write to the Director of Special Sales,
Professional Publishing, McGraw-Hill, Two Penn Plaza, New York, NY
10121-2298. Or contact your local bookstore.

This book is printed on acid-free paper.

Contents

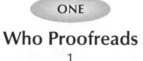

SIX

Giving Clear Instructions
53

SEVEN

Working with Type
71

EIGHT

Understanding the Typesetter's Language
85

APPENDIXES

Introduction

The written word is often the first impression a business makes on a prospective customer or client. If it isn't spelled right, if it isn't punctuated right, if it doesn't look good on paper, the business loses credibility.

Ideally, everything written in any office should be read for errors—typographical, spelling, grammatical, punctuation, and format—whether it is an annual report, an in-house publication, advertising copy, or a business letter. But even in those offices where the copy has been *read* for errors, mistakes slip through. More often than not, the reason this happens is because the copy was not *proofread* by a person trained for the job. There is a difference.

Some people, even aspiring proofreaders, do not understand what the word *proofreader* actually means, how proofreading differs from any other method of reading, or what distinguishes the proofreader from any other kind of reader. Following are definitions of all three: the title, the job, and the proofreader.

THE TITLE

Taken literally, the word *proofreader* is a present-day misnomer. The job dates from the advent of the printing press. "Proofs," or first impressions of printed copy, were pulled from the press so that the "proof reader" could check them for typographical errors. When the typewriter, then the computer, were invented, other kinds of "typos" weren't far behind. Because the task of reading for typed errors was virtually the same as reading for printed errors, the title *proofreader* stuck. So whether reading for errors on typed copy, on a desktop monitor, or on a reader's proof, laser print, or printer's proof, the one who performs the task is a proofreader.

THE JOB

In its most fundamental form, however, the job itself has changed. Computerized typing and typesetting, programmed with spelling and hyphenation checks, have encroached on the proofreader's original domain, threatening to eliminate those readers whose talents are limited to catching the most obvious mistakes.

But for the reader whose knowledge and interest lie beyond the eternal typo, computerization provides both relief and challenge. What was once a restrictive, often tedious occupation, is now an exciting opportunity to help ensure perfection through every step of the process and to become a far more valuable member of the communications team. For even the most sophisticated desktop equipment—now featuring grammar and punctuation checks, typesetting, and vast graphics capabilities—has not yet eliminated the need for a final, human stamp of approval. The system is still only as smart as the person who operates it. And proofreaders who capitalize on both its advantages and drawbacks not only increase their worth to the company but also widen their employment horizons immensely.

Technology has indisputably changed the proofreader's job requirements forever. As a result, employers are beginning to tighten their hiring standards. Proofreaders who can meet those expectations are being offered a higher salary and much more responsibility.

While proofreading is only one link in the "communications chain" (the progression of the written word from conception through production), the skills it requires are some of the most essential. The modern, state-of-the-art proofreader can save the company expense and embarrassment by catching a variety of obvious and not-so-obvious mistakes before they reach the costly stage of print—and ultimately the ever-critical eye of the intelligent reader.

THE PROOFREADER

Finding this kind of proofreader—or becoming one yourself—isn't easy. The job calls for technical knowledge of both language and print. It requires an aptitude, both inherent and acquired, for reading. And through each stage, it demands expertise and adaptability to the job at hand.

From typed concept to print, the copy passes through many stages and through numerous hands. And as is evident in the stages outlined below, the proofreader plays a central and essential role in the entire process, reading the copy for the different kinds of errors that can occur at each stage of development.

The following steps from the written to the printed word apply to many book- and magazine-length publications. Obviously, they will vary greatly from company to company or depending on the type of copy being proofread.

STAGE ONE
- The writer writes the copy.
- The editor edits or revises the copy.
- The editor or typist types the editor's changes to the copy.

STAGE TWO
- The designer creates type specifications and sends them to the typesetter.
- The typesetter sets the type and makes a reader's proof.
- The designer checks that the type specifications and layout were followed.
- The proofreader checks corrections, reads the entire proof for errors and consistency issues, and checks that the type specifications were followed.

STAGE THREE

- The typesetter makes corrections and sends back a revised proof.
- The proofreader (and the writer, editor, designer, client, and perhaps others) checks the corrections.
- This stage is repeated until the proofs are accurate and approved as final.

STAGE FOUR

- The production manager sends the electronic files with instructions to the printer.
- The printer makes negatives and sends a printer's proof ("bluelines") to the production manager.
- The production manager, editor, designer, proofreader, client, and perhaps others make a final check (mainly for dropped copy, correct page sequence, and things of that nature).

STAGE FIVE

- The copy is printed.

Because the proofreader must lend support to the writer, the editor, the typist, the designer, the typesetter, and the printer, you should have a basic understanding of the contribution of each, as well as the skills involved. The more you know about their roles, the better proofreader you will be. The proofreader's tools listed in Appendix A will help you achieve that goal. And, step by step, this book will guide you through the process.

Note that the words *typist* and *typesetter* are used frequently in these pages. The terms designate any person who types any part of the copy—the original text, the edited text, and subsequent rekeying or alterations of the text, layout, or type style in any way.

This book is not only for proofreaders but also for editors, writers, desktop publishers, and office managers—in fact, for everyone who strives for perfect copy.

For those who are not yet proofreaders, this book will explain the tasks and identify the skills that are needed to perform them. The chapters are mutually dependent, each one building upon the last. The beginner should read them in the order in which they appear. Study the book, use the tools recommended in the following pages, and practice your new skills at every opportunity.

For veterans of proofreading, this is an opportunity to enhance your skills, put more variety in your work, and get more satisfaction from it. The book may even reveal some secrets to proofreading you haven't already discovered.

ONE

Who Proofreads

THE WRITER AS PROOFREADER

Everyone is a proofreader, or at least most people go through the motions of proofreading every day. Whatever you have written or typed, there is a natural tendency to check it for accuracy. Chances are slim, though, that you will catch all your mistakes, even if you read it a second time.

Why? Any experienced proofreader—or a writer who has learned from experience—will be quick to tell you: *Don't proofread your own copy!* It's difficult to look at your own creative work with a critical or unbiased eye. You will, for the most part, see only what you expect to see.

Many writers work without the benefit of staff support. They must write, type, and proofread their own copy. If you work alone, put some distance between the time you write and when you proofread—hours, if not days. The longer you wait to re-read your copy, the greater your chances for a fresh, disinterested approach.

The real secret to proofreading your own copy is to read it slowly and critically, as though someone else had written it. It's hard to do, and that's why proofreaders are still in business.

THE ASSEMBLY-LINE PROOFREADER

In an office environment where there is no official proofreader, the job is most likely one shared among those involved in a project—the writer, the editor, and the creative director or project manager. It's logical that the more in-house exposure the copy gets, the more errors will be caught. So it should be read by as many people as possible, by some who are familiar with the material and, more importantly, by others who are not.

There are disadvantages to assembly-line proofreading. None of the readers may be trained to spot the many kinds of errors that can occur. Also, the lines of responsibility may become vague, creating a situation where no one is truly accountable for uncorrected errors.

If your office uses such a system, proceed with caution. Divide the proofreading duties outlined in these chapters among the readers, giving each a job in which he or she feels comfortable and has a certain degree of expertise. The best reader (most likely the editor, if there is one) should always be the last reader to look at the copy.

THE DESIGNATED READER

The ideal situation is to assign one qualified proofreader (or several, if the volume of written material is high), whose only job is to find and correct errors. This is where the buck truly stops. The trained proofreader catches either all the mistakes or the blame for missing them.

Managers may be tempted to designate a proofreader from among their present employees. This is a good idea, if there is such a person available with all the required skills. For the more familiar the proofreader already is with company policy and style, the more assured everyone will be of getting the job done quickly and correctly. If you are the one assigned this special duty, make sure that this new task preempts other duties. Ideally, other duties should be eliminated altogether, giving you the necessary time, solitude, and encouragement for thoughtful and accurate reading and inquiry.

If there is no one who is qualified and who can be relieved of other office chores, the manager will probably consider hiring a proofreader from outside the company. While past experience, good recommendations, an understanding of type and design, and preferably a degree in English are solid prerequisites for the job, many employers may also test for specific skills and knowledge, incorporating problems that are peculiar to their business. This is an excellent way to judge firsthand the expertise of applicants. If you are applying for a job as proofreader, you shouldn't be surprised if the prospective employer demands proof that you are the right one for the job.

IDENTIFYING YOUR SKILLS

What qualifies you as a proofreader may vary from business to business. And the duties you will have as proofreader may be just as unpredictable.

As a writer who must proofread your own work, you will have not only the privilege of complete authority but also the burden of complete responsibility, so your proofreading skills must be exceptional.

If you are one in a procession of assembly-line proofreaders within an office, you will correct as many errors as you know how to find and hope the other readers will catch what you missed. Or if duties have been divided among the readers, you will be responsible only for errors caught, and missed, in a particular area. Learn all you can about your assigned task. If you are not already an expert, work toward becoming one.

The skill requirements of the designated proofreader will be defined in the job description and will depend entirely on the particular needs of the business. You should understand those expectations before accepting the job and be prepared to meet them all.

LEVELS OF PROOFREADING

Beginner: Catches only deviations from the original copy, misspellings, incorrect math, incorrect word breaks, typing errors, and format style

Intermediate I: In addition to the duties of Beginner, catches grammatical and punctuation errors

Intermediate II: In addition to the duties of Intermediate I, is skilled in typeface identification and type specification

Intermediate III: In addition to the duties of Intermediate II, has advanced knowledge of language and type

Senior: In addition to the duties of Intermediate III, can perform some copyediting

MATCHING THE SKILLS TO THE JOB

The nature of a business signals implicit expectations about your skills. For example, in a publishing or editorial office, you will be expected to know (and care) more about word usage, grammar, and punctuation than in many other office environments. At a typesetting shop or printing company, you will often need more expertise in typeface identification, type specifications, and print production than you would need elsewhere. And at an advertising agency, you will often need both sets of skills in large measure.

These businesses make the greatest demands on their proofreaders. Also, working hours are often long and turnaround time is short. If the businesses don't produce perfect copy every time, they're in trouble. So they must hire the best and most experienced proofreaders they can find.

There is also a broad range of other businesses with an equally diverse range of expectations. So it is important that you know what kind of proofreading you do best, and what level of proofreading you have reached or aspire to reach.

Get as much information as possible about a prospective job before you accept it. You may be agreeing to more than you are qualified for or are interested in. Or you may become bored with the limitations imposed on you. Find a situation in which you will be most happy in terms of interest, skill requirements, authority, challenge, advancement, and salary. An underqualified, overqualified, or discontented proofreader is not a good proofreader.

TWO

Ways to Proofread

There are two ways to proofread, and how you do it is determined by what physical form the copy is in, as well as what stage of proofreading you have reached. Are you comparing one piece of typed or typeset copy against a previous version? Are you proofreading from a computer screen or a printout? Are you reading the copy for the first time, or are you re-reading it?

COMPARISON READING

When you compare two pieces of copy to make sure they are identical in every way, you are comparison reading. During this reading, you will make sure that the newly typed (or typeset) copy is exactly the same as the original, corrected text, in terms of word sequence and format. You will also watch for misspellings, bad word breaks, and typing mistakes at this stage, but you won't use this reading to create a style sheet or look for other errors or problems of style. That is the purpose of subsequent, noncomparison readings.

There are several ways to comparison read.

Reading Alone

You will compare the original manuscript (dead copy) with the newly typed version (live copy), or if the copy has reached the typeset stage, compare the typed copy (dead copy) with the typeset copy (live copy). The newest version of the copy is always con-

TABLE 2.1

Comparison Reading

Dead copy	*to be read against*	Live copy
Original copy		Typed copy
Typed copy		First galleys
First galleys		Revised galleys
Revised galleys		Final version

sidered the live copy. The copy you compare it with is the dead copy (see Table 2.1).

If you are right-handed, place the dead copy on your left and the live copy on your right. Left-handed proofreaders will place the dead copy on their right and the live copy on their left. In other words, the copy you will be correcting is always nearest the pen in your hand.

Place a nontransparent six-inch ruler under the line of the dead copy you are reading; place another ruler under the corresponding line in the live copy. This keeps your eyes focused on a single line of words instead of on the mass of lines below. It also keeps you from losing your place in case your reading is interrupted.

Now you are ready to begin. Read a few words from the dead copy, then read the corresponding words on the live copy. Continue reading from dead to live copy from beginning to end.

Reading with Another Person

This is a more efficient and interesting way to comparison read. The copyholder reads the dead copy aloud, word for word, including punctuation and format, while you proofread the live copy. Just as when you are comparison reading alone, you will read only for deviations from text and format, misspellings, typing errors, and incorrect word breaks. (For more details, see "Reading with the Copyholder" on page 10.)

Using a Tape Recorder

When there is no copyholder and the copy is long or difficult to read, a tape recording of the original (dead) copy will make comparison reading easier for you. As you record, you should read the copy slowly, enunciating every syllable, every punctuation mark, capitalization, paragraph beginning, and format instruction. Then proofread the live copy as you listen to the recorded version.

NONCOMPARISON (DRY OR SILENT) READING

There are times when the proofreader will have only one set of copy, the live copy, to read. There will be no dead copy to compare with your live copy. Or you may have already compared the two and are ready to move on to the second proofreading stage. You will be working alone at this stage, without the aid of dead copy, a copyholder, or a tape recorder. But you need not work quietly. Reading aloud, you will often hear mistakes that you might miss during a silent reading. Hearing the words produces a sharper mental image of them and how they are used.

After Comparison Reading

After the newly typed (or typeset) copy has been compared with the original text, your second, third, and any other passes will be those of noncomparison reading (except to check that corrections to the previous round were made). From these dry readings, you will follow the proofreading checklist (see page 20) and create a style sheet (see page 24).

On-Screen or on a Printout

Noncomparison reading is the only way to proofread when there is no dead copy to compare with the live copy, such as when you are proofreading from a computer screen or printout.

Desktop publishing equipment is now widespread in the office environment, and employees, including the proofreader, have their own computers, or workstations. These workstations are often linked via a server-based network and are used as copy relay stations among the writer, editor, and proofreader. As the copy is passed to each in such a direct fashion, comparison reading is useless. The computer screen *is* the copy. And a printed version (printout or hard copy) would be identical to what is on the screen.

A typical workflow is as follows: The writer composes the copy at a workstation, spell-checks, and perhaps even grammar-checks it, then electronically routes it to the editor's workstation. The editor has two choices in handling the material: (1) Editorial changes can be made on-screen, and the entire text is then routed to the proofreader's workstation for proofreading, or (2) the editor can create a printout of the on-screen text and mark editorial changes directly on the printout. Some editors prefer the latter method, since it provides a permanent record of the original copy and the editorial changes. Modern word-processing software, however, permits changes to be tracked in electronic documents.

Access to a workstation gives the proofreader the same two choices. If the copy is electronically routed to the proofreader, corrections and queries can be made on-screen. Long queries or explanations can be incorporated directly in the text, to be dealt with (and deleted) later by the writer or editor.

On-screen proofreading can be more difficult than proofreading from a printout: You may "lose your place" more easily when reading on-screen, and lengthy on-screen reading can be tiring. These disadvantages can be outweighed by the speed and ease of correcting on-screen. For example, if you spot an error that you think may be repeated throughout the document, you can perform a global search-and-replace operation and be assured that you have found all instances of the error. In addition, on-screen proofreading enables you to make changes on the spot, not merely mark them for later entry.

Because on-screen proofreading is so convenient, however, you may be tempted to "correct" something that, on a printout, you would have only questioned. Yielding to this temptation could cause trouble. What you suspect is an error could be intentional by the writer. Be sure to insert queries on all important changes you make.

Once the copy is typeset, using a printout is standard procedure for subsequent editing and proofreading. Actually, it's foolhardy at this stage for a typesetter to give access to electronic files to any writer, editor, or proofreader. Hard copy is required so that later proofreaders can keep track of what changes were made at every stage.

After the editing and proofreading have been performed either on-screen or on a printout (and, in the latter case, have been made to the document file), a final hard copy should be printed out. This copy is then read by the writer, the editor, and the proofreader. (If corrections were made on-screen, you will read by the noncomparison method; if corrections were marked on a printout, then keyed in, you will read by the comparison method.) Make sure all changes and corrections have been made. And watch for new errors entered accidentally when the old ones were corrected.

BACK TO COMPARISON READING

This hard copy now becomes the dead copy and the proofreader will use it for comparison reading at the next stage, making sure that the typeset proof is identical to the hard copy, the revised proof matches the typeset proof, and the final version is the same as the typeset proof. After the initial comparison reading with the dead copy at each stage, re-readings of the live copy will be non-comparison readings.

As the job progresses from the typed to the typeset stage, errors will be more expensive to correct. So make sure you catch them as they occur at each stage.

READING WITH THE COPYHOLDER

The copyholder is valuable to a busy proofreader, especially when the text is long or handwritten, or if it contains many editorial changes or rows of numbers.

There are no extraordinary skills required for the job except an ability to read aloud and distinctly. The copyholder can be anyone you are lucky enough to enlist, from the mail room clerk to the editor in chief. Most often, an administrative or editorial assistant is selected for this special duty.

The procedure is simple. While you concentrate on the live copy, the copyholder reads the dead copy aloud to you, articulating every syllable, spelling words if necessary, noting punctuation marks, capitalization, and format instructions. This voice-and-scan process eliminates your having to juggle both the original text and the newly typed or typeset copy, an awkward procedure in which you could easily miss a deviation from the original text.

Voice Rhythm

The copyholder should speak clearly and as slowly as the proofreader thinks is necessary, repeating words, phrases, or entire sections if you need them re-read. The copyholder should strive for a smooth, unbroken reading rhythm, avoiding unnecessary stops and starts and erratic pauses, and resisting interruptive and irrelevant comments about the copy. The copyholder should pause only when you have stopped proofreading to make a correction.

Unfamiliar or Foreign Words

Although the copyholder may be tempted to pronounce an unfamiliar or foreign word, what may seem the correct pronunciation to the copyholder may be quite different from the way the word should actually be pronounced. The copyholder should not pause when these words appear, or attempt to pronounce them, but instead spell them out letter by letter. In the case of foreign words, accent marks (diacritics) should also be indicated to the proofreader by the copyholder.

Copyholder's Vocabulary

Just as the proofreader uses a unique language to communicate (proofreader's marks), the copyholder also has a special way of communicating. It is an abbreviated way of reading numerals (to distinguish them from spelled-out numbers), punctuation marks, underscores, capital letters, copy layout, and typeface changes. Using the copyholder's vocabulary is, of course, optional, but the clarity and speed it provides are worth the effort to learn it. A little practice makes it easy, and it will soon become an indispensable tool for both the copyholder and the proofreader. The most common "words" are listed in Table 2.2. Following is a sample of copy as seen and heard by the proofreader.

The copy as it looks to the proofreader

Whether you're still in school or you head up a corporation, the better command you have of words, the better chance you have of saying exactly what you mean, of understanding what others mean—and of getting what you want in the world.

English is the richest language—with the largest vocabulary—on earth. Over 1,000,000 words!

You can express shades of meaning that aren't even *possible* in other languages. (For example, you can differentiate between "sky" and "heaven." The French, Italians, and Spanish cannot.)*

The copy as it sounds to the proofreader

whether you pos r e still in school or you head up a corporation com the better command you have of words com the better chance

---

*Randall, Tony. "How to Improve Your Vocabulary," *Power of the Printed Word* series. New York: International Paper Company, 1982.

TABLE 2.2

The Copyholder's Vocabulary

Plain English	Copyholder's term
Punctuation	
apostrophe	pos
bracket	brack . . . close brack
bullet	spot
colon	cole
comma	com
dash (length)	em dash/en dash
ellipsis	three dots
ellipsis with period	four dots
exclamation point	bang
hyphen	hy OR hook
two hyphens	two hooks
(as in "word-for-word")	
parenthesis	pren . . . close pren
period	dot OR stop
question mark	huh OR hey
quotation mark	quote . . . unquote
semicolon	semi
slash	slash OR slant
swung dash (~)	snake
Symbols	
ampersand (&)	et
asterisk (*)	astrik
cents symbol (¢)	cee slash
copyright mark (©)	cee mark
dagger (†)	dag
degree mark (°)	ball
dollar symbol ($)	buck
double dagger (‡)	two dag
percent mark (%)	two balls
registration mark (®)	ar mark
star (★)	star

TABLE 2.2 (continued)

Plain English	Copyholder's term
Letters and Numbers	
the letter o	oh
the numeral 0	num zero
the numeral 12	num one two OR fig one two
twenty-four	twenty hy four
hundred (two zeros)	hun
thousand (three zeros)	thou
million (six zeros)	mil
decimal point	point
Type Style	
roman type	rome
italic type	ital . . . end ital
boldface type	bold . . . end bold
underlined type	rule . . . end rule
lowercase word	elsie OR one down, two down (etc.)
all-capitalized words	caps OR all-cap
first-letter cap	one up, two up (etc.) OR click
inferior character	sub
superior character	supe
new paragraph	new pare OR graph
indent	dent
indent two spaces or two ems	dent two (etc.)

Accents (Diacritics)

Example	Copyholder's term	Example	Copyholder's term
í	acute	ç	cedilla
è	grave	ł	stroke
ő	double acute	â	circumflex
ā	macron	ñ	tilde
š	caron OR hachek	đ	crossbar
ø	slash	ü	umlaut OR dieresis

you have of saying exactly what you mean com of understanding what others mean em dash and of getting what you want in the world dot new pare english is the richest language em dash with the largest vocabulary em dash on earth dot over fig one com thou com thou words bang new pare ital you end ital can express shades of meaning that are n pos t even ital possible end ital in other languages dot pren for example com you can differentiate between quote sky unquote and quote heaven dot unquote the french one up com italians one up com and spanish one up cannot dot close pren

It is not necessary for the copyholder to say "one up" for a capital letter at the beginning of a sentence. But if there is the likelihood of the proofreader misunderstanding any of these short-cut terms during the course of the reading, the copyholder will explain them in plain English. Clarity should not be sacrificed to speed.

THREE

Proofreading Skills

APTITUDE

There is a common misconception that anyone who can read, can proofread. But those who have accepted a job or have hired someone on that premise know better. There is literally more to proofreading than meets the eye.

> According to management theory, our school system produces more ready-made proofreaders than there is a demand for. Only underpaid readers really believe this. The fact is that there is an aptitude requirement for reading, just as there is for music, mechanics or math. . . . Anyone with the capability and inclination to accept the discipline of proofreading is a rare find. The fact is, a good proofreader has an aptitude for reading.*

An aptitude for reading is, indeed, a prerequisite to good proofreading. Certainly one who doesn't like to read will not like to proofread. Even someone who enjoys reading may not enjoy proofreading *or* be good at it. There are other skills that the serious proofreader is motivated to develop and that supplement the natural inclinations one may possess (Table 3.1).

DEVELOPING THE RIGHT ATTITUDE

Proofreading is a very intimidating and stressful occupation. Anyone who has ever done it knows why. The job requirements simply

---

*McNaughton, Harry H. *Proofreading and Copyediting*. New York: Hastings House, 1973.

TABLE 3.1

Learned Skills

Developing the right attitude
Knowing how to read
Knowing what to look for
Remembering what you read
Understanding the writer's language
Querying decisively and effectively
Giving clear instructions
Working with type
Understanding the typesetter's language

---

defy nature. Hired to ensure perfect copy, the proofreader must catch everyone else's mistakes and not *make* one in the process. No matter whose error it might have been initially, the proofreader is ultimately responsible. Unquestionably, anxiety comes with the territory. You should prepare yourself (and your ego) for the inevitable error, while at the same time doing everything possible to avoid it.

Here are some ways to ease the tension while you read.

Clear the Room

You can't be sociable and proofread at the same time, so don't talk to others while you are trying to concentrate. Ringing telephones are another major nuisance. Even anticipating a telephone call will interfere with your ability to concentrate. A quiet place to work is essential to good proofreading.

Clear the Cobwebs

Fatigue or boredom creates distraction. If you are not totally focused on your work for either of these reasons, you will make errors. Count on it.

FATIGUE

Lengthy copy or long working hours don't necessarily condemn a reader to hours of unbroken concentration. Work breaks certainly help. Dividing your work into segments is a much more productive approach.

BOREDOM

Proofreading can be tedious when the copy is not interesting, when it is badly written, and especially when revisions of the same copy rc-appear on your desk. But you can train yourself to be energetic and interested in whatever you are reading. If the copy isn't fascinating to read or doesn't offer an opportunity to learn, make it a challenge in another way. For example, make proofreading a game. Look for errors, and you are bound to find them. Subtle ones are just as important as, and definitely more fun and satisfying to catch than, obvious ones. The more errors you know how to look for (in language and in the type itself), the more you will find, and the more enjoyable and relaxed proofreading will be.

KNOWING HOW TO READ

Read the Instructions

You'll avoid numerous false starts, unnecessary questions, and mistakes if you read the instructions (if any) first. The writer or designer may have already anticipated your questions and included a guide for you. Try not to interrupt these people with queries that have already been answered in the instructions. But if the information is confusing or unclear, do seek clarification before you begin the job. (See also Appendix B, "McGraw-Hill's General Instructions for Freelance Proofreaders.")

Read Methodically

Always comparison read first—with a copyholder, a tape recorder, or alone—word for word at least once at each stage: typed manuscript, typeset galleys, and printer's proof. Then read the live copy again as many additional times as it takes to create your style sheet and to complete your tasks. When there is no dead text to compare, read the copy aloud, then read it again (and again) until you are confident that all errors have been found.

Read Slowly

People who are adept at speed-reading will never succeed at proofreading when those particular skills are employed. Read at a comfortable, deliberate pace. Don't allow a tight schedule or impatient co-workers to rush you. If you don't have the time to read the copy critically and slowly, wait until you do.

Read with Rhythm

Reading slowly doesn't always mean that you must read from letter to letter, unless that is the method you are most comfortable with. There are two exceptions: When you are reading very small or very large type or when you are reading foreign-language copy, you will have a much better chance of catching all the mistakes if you stop to look carefully at each letter.

Neither do you have to read from word to word, once the first-time comparison reading has been completed. The pace of subsequent readings can accelerate to a moderate speed through a series of eye stops across a line of print. The eyes move along, stop to let in the light needed to see an image, then move on to the next eye stop. With practice, you can see two words per eye stop, and sometimes three words, depending on the length of the words.

First, focus your eyes on one word—the whole word, if possible. Now try two. Find the most comfortable span for your eyes, and practice reading this way. Your vision should flow, not jump, from one eye stop to the next. Keep the rhythm of the flow to the end of the line.

If your eye span is too short to take in an entire word or two, practice reading by word syllables. Expanding your eye stops will automatically produce speed. More importantly, it will produce a steadier rhythm.

Contrary to what some occasional proofreaders believe, reading the copy backward is unnecessary torture and, if you are a full-time proofreader, a painful way to earn a living. Many proofreaders who insist on this method eventually disappear from the trade altogether.

Look for Red Flags

Reading methodically, slowly, and with rhythm works most of the time. But there are some places in the copy that should send warning signals for an even closer look:

- Copy that *you* have written or typed
- Revised copy
- Long lines of type
- Short lines of type
- Double consonants or vowels
- A series of narrow letters (for example, *ili*, *ifi*, and *til*)
- All-capitalized letters
- Large display type
- Small type
- Black letter or ornamental type
- Sans serif type
- Italicized letters
- Numerals: decimal points, commas, alignment, and totals
- Pairs of parentheses, quote marks, brackets, or dashes

KNOWING WHAT TO LOOK FOR

There are many stages between the original text and the printed word, and there are proofreading hazards every step of the way.

Keeping in mind all the different kinds of errors you are looking for (and finding them all in the brief amount of time you will have to read) comes from experience.

Proofreading Checklists

The wise beginner will categorize proofreading duties in a logical order, then separate them by readings. You will need a list for every stage of production (see Appendix C, "Proofreading Check-lists"). You won't need the lists forever, but refer to them for as long as you do. Soon the routine should become second nature.

The lists suggested in Appendix C may be insufficient or excessive or not in your preferred groupings. Your own lists will depend on the nature of the copy you are reading and the limit of your responsibility and authority. You may want to combine some of the readings or divide them even further, with one exception. Even the pros—especially the pros—separate mechanical (format) tasks from reading tasks. You don't have to confine your readings to a certain number of passes. Just read until you feel the job is done.

Following the list as you read, you will undoubtedly spot errors you are not looking for during that particular reading. Mark errors *when* you see them. Don't wait until you are scheduled to, because you might then overlook them.

Common Errors

You also might want to keep a list of the most common errors:

- Incorrectly spelled names
- Transposed numbers in addresses and telephone numbers
- Incorrect dates
- Incorrect capitalization
- Doubly typed words or phrases
- Omissions of words or parts of words
- Incorrect or missing punctuation

- Nonagreement of subject and verb
- Misspelled words

Other Tips

- Sometimes when you find one error, you may find a whole nest of them nearby.
- Apparent errors that recur could be intentional misspellings or unusual usages, so ask or check the style sheet before you begin making unnecessary corrections.
- Watch for words that are commonly misused or misspelled or that sound alike but have different meanings and spellings (see Appendix D, "Words and Phrases Commonly Confused or Misused").
- Watch for changes in typeface or type size.
- Make sure bibliographic entries are alphabetical, that authors' names and titles are spelled correctly, and that bibliographic elements are in their proper order and punctuated correctly. Bibliographies should be carefully proofread against the original text.
- Check titles, subtitles, charts, and page numbers against the table of contents. Check any page references within the text, making sure that the referenced material is on the page indicated.

FOUR

Remembering What You Read

Proofreading is never a routine occupation. Even during a second or third pass, you will inevitably discover some error or inconsistency that you missed the first time around. Keep alert, and you will be able to eliminate some of those repeated readings. Concentrate, and you will remember much of what you have read.

While it's necessary to cultivate a good memory for detail, inconsistencies, and repetition, you don't have to remember everything. Just know where to find what you are looking for. A stylebook or style sheet is one of the best reminders a proofreader can have. This has nothing to do with literary style. It's a set of rules or guidelines intended to ensure consistency of format, spelling, capitalization, abbreviations, word usage, and other technicalities peculiar to the copy you are reading.

THE STYLEBOOK

Published stylebooks are commercially available and are excellent resources for general office use. Designed for a specific group of writers and editors (and proofreaders), they have quickly spread in popularity beyond the particular community for which they were originally intended.

For example, *The New York Times* mandates style standards that must be followed by all of its writers. So does the U.S. government in its stylebook. And *The Chicago Manual of Style* has long been a respected source of style for academic writers. There are many other such publications, varying in content and emphasis, and one of them will likely be appropriate for your office.

Editors usually decide which stylebook will be used, or they will establish a style themselves. In an office where there is no editor or book or style to follow, the proofreader should request one, be permitted to choose or develop a standard, or create a style sheet that follows the predominant style, assuming it is a correct one, of the copy being read.

THE STYLE SHEET

The style sheet is not a random listing of points to be remembered while reading copy—it is much more calculated and organized than that. Otherwise, you will not easily find the information without searching through the entire list each time. You could spend as much (or more) time searching for style as you would reading copy. A style sheet is intended to save time and trouble. Know what points of style to look for (see Table 4.1), faithfully maintain a style

TABLE 4.1

Points of Style

Format
Spelling and capitalization
Hyphenations
Numerals
Plurals, possessives, and punctuation
Abbreviations
Special treatment
Dates
Foreign words
Facts
Trademarks and service marks, copyright marks, and logotypes
Footnotes, bibliographies, tables, and charts
Miscellaneous

sheet that reflects the style of the copy you are reading, and refer to the style sheet as often as you need to. (See "Designing Your Style Sheet" on page 37.)

Format

If the physical appearance (layout) of the copy has not already been specified, either through office policy or by the editor or designer, format will be identified by glancing through the copy, measuring its dimensions, and writing them down on the style sheet. For future reference, attach to the style sheet samples of work—memos, conference reports, business letters, manuscripts, newsletters, or any other copy formats that will be referred to again. Seeing how the copy should actually look is much easier than having to measure copy each time. (See Table 4.2.)

TABLE 4.2

Format: Typed and Typeset Copy

Typed copy format for each style element
Typeface
Size of type
Margins (top, bottom, left, and right)
Spacing (between lines and paragraphs)
Tabs and other indents
Position of heads and subheads
Computer file format or style name (if applicable)

Typeset copy format for each style element
Typeface
Size of type
Weight, width, and posture of type
Leading
Margins
Other special measurements

Spelling and Capitalization

It is important that you include on the style sheet the exact spelling and capitalization of proper nouns (names, places, and organizations), noting carefully anything unusual. For example, if it's *Mr. Jonathan Smythe* you are reading about, make sure he doesn't become *Mr. John Smith* later in the copy. And if you first read, then record *U.S. Postal Service* (after making sure it *is* the proper usage), you will know that *U.S. Post Office* or *post office,* which may appear later in the copy, should be changed or at least questioned. If *The Peoples and Southeast Mortgage Corporation* (note the cap *T* and lowercase *and*) is referred to later as *the P&S Mortgage Corporation* (note the lowercase *t* and *&*), either reference may be correct. You will remember the details if they are entered in the style sheet. You will also know what to do if *P&S* later appears as *P & S* (note the added spaces).

To avoid having to search through the copy each time you encounter an apparent inconsistency, first determine the proper spelling or capitalization or spacing (by asking the editor, finding the answer yourself, or using the predominant style). Then write it down legibly in the appropriate place on your style sheet. You will have to look no further than your style sheet the next time you have a style question.

Another important point to remember is that sometimes words may be spelled in two ways (*toward/towards, database/data base*). Dictionaries often list a preference. According to *The American Heritage Dictionary* (second college edition), *"judgment also judgement"* (note *also*) are both generally accepted but the first spelling is preferred; and although both *"ax or axe"* (note *or*) are accepted, there is no preference of one over the other. (Be sure to consult the guide in the dictionary you are using; some may indicate a preference differently.) When there is no preference, it is the writer's or editor's choice. Get into the habit of looking for, or asking about, these special words.

Hyphenations

Often words are hyphenated when used either as compound adjectives or compound nouns before nouns that they modify (*full-service* or *decision-making*) but are not hyphenated when they are used together as a noun phrase (*full service* or *decision making*). If you get confused or if the copy isn't consistent, ask the writer or editor. Some use hyphens more sparingly than others. Or follow the predominant style.

List on the style sheet all the compound words that have potential for creating hyphenation problems for you later on. Such a list will be especially helpful if you are reading long copy.

Hyphens can create confusion in other ways, such as when the first letters of all main words are capitalized (called initial caps) and one of those words is hyphenated. The word before the hyphen is capitalized, but what about the word following the hyphen? *Re-read This Copy* or *Re-Read This Copy*? The editor or designer may choose to initial-cap *Read,* because it looks better that way.

Another decision must be made when similar words are used in a series and the dictionary recognizes some of them as hyphenated words and some as nonhyphenated words:

> The writer must *re-read* and *rewrite,* or *replace,* the copy and *re-position* it on the page.

This creates a visually unattractive line and it often becomes a style decision, rather than a matter of correct hyphenation, to avoid creating undue attention. The editor may choose either to hyphenate all of them or, more likely, to eliminate the hyphens altogether.

There are many such decisions that will be made based on style rather than correctness. Although you will not make these decisions, at least note them on your style sheet. You will feel much more comfortable knowing why rules are sometimes broken. And soon you will be able to recognize and point out potential troublemakers such as these.

Numerals

There is no single official rule or style for writing numerals, although there are some commonly preferred ones among those who write or publish for a living.

Numerical tables and columns of numbers are almost always expressed in digits. When numbers appear randomly throughout the copy, most journalists use a standardized style of writing out as words numbers *one* through *nine,* and as figures *10* and above. An accepted variation of this is spelling out *one* through *ninety-nine,* then using numerical figures for *100* and above. The writer or editor may choose one of these styles, use all digits, or spell them all out—whichever style looks best and appropriate for a particular piece of copy.

Watch for inconsistent treatment of numbers used monetarily (such as *10¢, $.10, ten cents, 10 cents*) and make sure they are all treated uniformly. A style should also be determined for percentages (*10%, ten percent, 10 percent*).

Plurals, Possessives, and Punctuation

There are grammatical rules that help the writer or editor decide how to treat plural and possessive words. (In advertising copy, the writer may also be guided by client preference. See "Special Treatment" on page 30.) There is sometimes a choice of style, however, and you should know the rules well enough to maintain consistency throughout the copy. Here are a few examples of plural and possessive treatment:

LETTERS   L's—ALSO Ls
             a's, e's, i's—NOT as, es, is
             A's, E's, I's—NOT As, Es, Is

WORDS	do's and don'ts—NOT dos OR don't's
	if's, and's, or but's—ALSO ifs, ands, or buts
	miss's—NOT misss
	Davis's house—ALSO Davis' house
	Chris's money—BUT ALSO Chris' salary
	Joe's and Janc's cars
	Joe and Jane's car—ALSO Joe's and Jane's car
NUMERALS	7's OR 7s
SYMBOLS	&'s OR &s
ACRONYMS	UFO's OR UFOs
	Ph.D.'s—NOT Ph.D.s
DATES	1800's OR 1800s

Punctuation is editorial territory, but the more familiar you are with the rules, the better able you will be to spot an error when you encounter one. Except for a few choices (such as hyphenation, the use of the apostrophe as shown above, or adding a comma after an introductory phrase or before a conjunction in a series), there is no punctuation "style." Copy is either punctuated right or punctuated wrong. And most writers or editors will not take too many liberties with the rules if they want to be understood. Making sure that punctuation is exactly as they want it is your job. Understanding why makes the job more enjoyable.

Abbreviations

Abbreviations are not always treated consistently by writers. And that can be a problem for the proofreader. The best advice is to look up the abbreviation in either a comprehensive dictionary or a published stylebook, then write it down in the appropriate alphabetized section of your style sheet. Sometimes there is more than one way to abbreviate a word or group of words. In the absence of an editor, the proofreader chooses the most common style evident in the copy and uses it as the guide for all abbreviations. Some examples follow:

STATES	Conn. OR CT, Neb. OR NE, N.Y. OR NY
DIRECTION	N.W., NW, OR NW.
ACADEMIC DEGREES	Ph.D., A.B., B.S., M.B.A.
	—NOT PhD, AB, BS, MBA
TIMES OF DAY	A.M., A.M., OR a.m.; P.M., P.M., OR p.m.
TITLES	C.P.A. OR CPA, F.B.I. OR FBI

Some abbreviations are not so straightforward. Abbreviations for some common nouns, such as *public service announcement* (*PSA*), *physical education* (*PE*), and *account executive* (*AE*), are capitalized, while others, such as for *government* (*gov.* or *govt.*) and *afternoon (aft.)*, are lowercase. Watch the caps and the periods. Look them up and monitor use carefully.

There are still other abbreviated words to watch out for, words the average reader (but not the average proofreader) may fail to notice. The nonword *'til* is often used as an abbreviation of *until*. Most experts—but not all—still agree that the correct abbreviation is *till*, no matter how illogical it may appear. Look at the different abbreviations for the word *and: 'n, n', or 'n'*. In most cases, the accepted rule is to use an apostrophe wherever a letter or letters are omitted.

An abbreviation that should be questioned by the proofreader is the nonword *thru* for *through*. A dash (—) or ellipsis (. . .) is often incorrectly used as a substitute for commas, semicolons, or end marks. This is especially common in advertising copy. But most proofreaders don't get too entangled in enforcing these rules if they are not important to the editor. In your query, cite the rule (and the reference), then follow the editor's decision consistently throughout.

Special Treatment

If the end justifies the means, any writer may deliberately deviate from commonly accepted style, spell a word differently than it appears in the dictionary, capitalize an ordinarily lowercase word

TABLE 4.3

Advertising Deviations from Spelling or Grammar

American Express® Travelers Cheque™
Diet Rite® (cola)
More cheesier (Kraft Macaroni & Cheese Dinner)
America's Most BTU-tiful Fuel℠
UnflappaBull
Dr Pepper®
Heat 'N Serve®

Travelers Cheque is a trademark of American Express Ltd. *Diet Rite* is a registered trademark of Royal Crown Company Inc. *More cheesier* was an advertising slogan used by Kraft, Inc. *America's Most BTU-tiful Fuel* was a service mark of the American Gas Association. *UnflappaBull* was an advertising term used by Bull HN Information Systems Inc. *Dr Pepper* is a registered trademark of Dr Pepper/ Seven Up, Inc. *Heat 'N Serve* was a registered trademark of Sara Lee Foods, Inc.

or lowercase a traditionally capitalized word, make up new words, deviate from rules of grammar and punctuation, or do anything else that will make the copy unique. Special treatment is quite evident in advertising copy as an attention-getting device or simply because the client wants it that way. (See examples in Table 4.3.) If you must work with this kind of copy on a day-to-day basis, get familiar with the deviations. And if you can't remember all of them, let the style sheet do it for you.

Dates

Dates may be written in a variety of styles, so find the most prevalent one, ask the editor, or establish one yourself. Any of the following styles are acceptable; all you must do is ensure consistency.

- 18th century; eighteenth century (adjective and noun)
- 18th-century; eighteenth-century (compound adjective)
- 1900's; 1900s
- October 1989; October, 1989; Oct. 1989; Oct., 1989; 10/89

- January 10, 1976; 10 January 1976; Jan. 10, 1976; 10 Jan. 1976; 01/10/76 (preferred over 1/10/76)

Remember, if a comma precedes the year, another comma must follow if it is not at the end of a sentence. An example is "His first book was published June 1, 1988, and was a best seller." Also correct is "His first book was published in June 1988 and was a best seller."

Foreign Words

It is rare that copy written in English will contain more than a scattering of foreign words or phrases. List all that are used in the copy on the style sheet, noting accent marks and their positioning over or under the letters. Americans are not accustomed to accent marks and occasionally will put them in the wrong place or at the wrong angle or neglect them altogether. They *are* relevant. All foreign words (except those already adopted by Americans, such as "avant-garde" or "hors d'oeuvre") should be italicized or underscored. Also keep in mind that even words in the English language may be spelled differently, depending on which side of the Atlantic Ocean you're proofreading.

Facts

In copy that you read, the subject matter may not be familiar to you. And in long manuscripts, it is difficult to remember or record all the facts stated. It isn't as hard remembering the facts in advertising copy, especially if the client (and you) have been with the agency for a long time.

Although the proofreader is not usually liable for any factual misinformation or inconsistencies, your careful attention to detail would be welcomed by all. Write down on your style sheet what facts you do learn from reading the copy. As an experienced proofreader, you will develop almost a sixth sense for those facts you will most likely need to remember. An example in advertising copy: ". . . fourteen offices throughout the city"—followed by a list of only 12 addresses later in the copy or even in another advertisement.

Trademarks and Service Marks

In any nonfictional copy, watch for trademarks (™), service marks (SM), and registration marks (®) and list them beside the product name in the style sheet. One mark cannot be substituted for another mark.

The Trademark Act of 1946 defines a trademark as follows:

> The term "trademark" includes any word, name, symbol, or device or any combination thereof adopted and used by a manufacturer or merchant to identify his goods and distinguish them from those manufactured by others. (15 U.S.C. 1127)

The Trademark Act of 1946 defines a service mark as follows:

> The term "service mark" means a mark used in the sale or advertising of services to identify the services of one person and distinguish them from the services of others. (15 U.S.C. 1127)

If either a trademark or service mark is registered in the U.S. Patent and Trademark Office, the 1946 Trademark Act requires that it must be followed by one of three forms of notice:

1. Registered in U.S. Patent and Trademark Office.
2. Reg. U.S. Pat. & Tm. Off.
3. ®

The symbol ® is most often used as a notice of a mark's registration. If a mark isn't registered in the U.S. Patent and Trademark

Office, it is protected under common law of the states when one of the following common law marks is used:

1. ™ (a common law mark that is a trademark)
2. ℠ (a common law mark that is a service mark)

A common law mark may become registered in the U.S. Patent and Trademark Office. When that happens, the ™ or ℠ will become ®.

These marks are public, legal notices to the reader that the company wants to protect its product and service names from encroachment by another company. There is no legal obligation to use these symbols, and some stylebooks recommend not including them. But if the marks aren't used consistently and correctly in advertisements or in other communications (even internal communications), or if the company doesn't take steps to preserve those rights when others use the name without permission, those rights could be lost and the product or service name could become a generic term and, consequently, common property of anyone who wants to use it.

In advertising copy, names of products belonging to the client will usually bear one of these marks to identify ownership. Unless specifically instructed to do otherwise, you should make sure that a mark follows the product name once per page, usually at its first mention or in its most prominent position. Sometimes, too, depending on client preference, a footnote appears at the bottom of the page or at the end of the copy as an additional means of identifying the product owner.

Products or services that are the property of a company other than your client are sometimes mentioned in the advertisement as well. They must be similarly marked in the copy and always identified in a footnote.

The common format to footnote a product that is a registered trademark is as follows:

Widget is a registered trademark of the ABC Company.

Since a trademark or service mark will be positioned beside the name Widget in the body of the copy, it is not necessary to place another mark beside it in the footnote.

Company names also may be registered as trade names (not marks) and are accompanied by a registration mark if they are used as adjectives modifying a word that describes a type of product or service. Used alone, as a noun, a company name does not require a mark notice, unless it is used with the registered logotype. For example, when the company name American Express is used alone, as a noun, it is not followed by a registration mark. When it is used as an adjective modifying one of its products or services, it is followed by a registration mark (American Express® Travelers Cheque™). And when it appears beside the logo (often at the bottom of the advertisement), it will most likely be accompanied by a registration or common law mark.

Copyright Marks

Another footnote is standard on all published copy to protect it from being used in any way without permission of the copyright owner. Copyright lines are included in all books, magazine articles, and brochures, as well as in most advertisements. The date of the copyright is the date the article was first published. If the copy is changed or altered in any way, it becomes "new copy" and the copyright must be updated accordingly to reflect the new material. The proofreader should remember to check the inclusion of a copyright line and make sure that the date and copyright owner's name are correct.

© 1989 ABC Company
Copyright 1989 ABC Company
copr. 1989 ABC Company

A trademark or service mark that fits the definition of a "work" under the Copyright Act may also be copyrighted. Some foreign countries do not recognize marks other than the copyright mark, so it is used for protection against international infringement.

Logotypes

The corporate logo is commonly used on any printed material that is published by a corporation or by an advertising agency on behalf of its client. Often registered in the U.S. Patent and Trademark Office, the logo consists of the corporate name and a corporate symbol (both usually in a special typeface and design). It is positioned somewhere on the page or advertisement, usually at the bottom, above the legal footnotes. Logos are carefully designed to create a visual image of the corporation, one that a casual reader of the advertisement will remember long after the words in the advertisement have been forgotten. Logos and their accompanying registration mark are essential items in the proofreader's style sheet and on the proofreader's checklist.

Footnotes, Bibliographies, Tables, and Charts

You will follow the style set by the writer or editor. Write at least one example of each on the style sheet and refer to the examples for style and consistency.

Miscellaneous

There will often be points that you will want to remember but cannot categorize in the style sheet: facts, addresses, telephone numbers, scientific or legal terms, and so on. A "Miscellaneous" section will serve as a catchall for those odds and ends that you may need to compare as you progress through the copy.

You may not use all the suggested points of style in some copy you will be reading. Or you may want to add a few new ones to the style sheet you compile for other jobs. Design or modify your style sheet so that it will accommodate you and the copy you are reading. Alphabetize the points in each section—a time-saver during future reference.

DESIGNING YOUR STYLE SHEET

Take several sheets of paper, preferably 8½ inches by 11 inches for easy handling, copying, distributing, and filing. You are going to alphabetize items, so draw or type enough sections on the sheets to include each letter of the alphabet (X, Y, and Z items can usually be combined into one section). Create additional sections for points that can't be alphabetized (punctuation and style, footnotes and references, special symbols, treatment of numerals, typing format, and typographic style). (See Table 4.4 for an example.) You may also wish to indicate a specific dictionary to use for word breaks.

For some proofreading jobs, the narrow ruled boxes may not provide sufficient space to record all the points you need to remember. You may feel less confined with the ruled lines that extend the full width of the page (Table 4.5).

General Office Style Sheet

The simplest style sheet is a compilation of predetermined general standards by which every piece of written or typed copy emanating from the office is compared. This includes memos, business correspondence, annual reports, and everything in between. You may want a separate style sheet for each. The wide box style sheet may be more suitable for these points than the narrow box style sheet. (See Appendix E for examples of general office style sheets.)

The style sheet(s) can be sketchy or elaborately detailed, but at least the basics should be included, such as format instructions, spacing, capitalization, spelling of frequently used words (such as

Text continues on page 42.

TABLE 4.4

Narrow Box Style Sheet

Trademarks Registration Marks Service Marks Logos Copyrights Other Legal	Typing Format	Type Specifications
Special Usage/ Placement	Numerical Style	Miscellaneous Facts/ Notes

TABLE 4.4 (continued)

Capitalization Hyphenation Italics Possessives Punctuation Spelling (adj) adjective (cn) collective noun (dict) dictionary preference (n) noun (pa) predicate adj (pl) plural (poss) possessive (sing) singular (v) verb	A	B
C	D	E
F	G	H (and so on)

TABLE 4.5

Wide Box Style Sheet

Trademarks/Logos
Registration Marks/Legal
Special Usage/Placement
Typing Format
Type Specifications
Numerical Style

TABLE 4.5 (continued)

Capitalization/Hyphenation/Italics/Possessives/Punctuation/Spelling
(adj) adjective   (pl) plural (cn) collective noun   (poss) possessive (dict) dictionary preference   (sing) singular (n) noun   (v) verb (pa) predicate adj
A
B
C (and so on)
Footnotes, Bibliographies, and Tables
Miscellaneous Facts/Notes

proper nouns), treatment of numerals—in short, whatever should be considered standard office policy. Organized by subject matter, this style sheet should be typed and distributed to every employee. Additions, deletions, and any changes should be made promptly and re-circulated to office workers.

Manuscript Style Sheet

Another kind of style sheet is primarily used for book manuscripts or any copy that, as far as the proofreader is aware, has no pre-determined editorial style. It is created during the actual reading. (See Appendix F for examples.)

In book publishing, the copy editor will create a style sheet that the proofreader will follow and add to, if necessary. This style sheet will accompany the project through all stages of production.

Only in very unusual circumstances will the proofreader set style, and this will be by identifying the style that most often occurs in the text.

Once style has been established and recorded on the style sheet, everyone who subsequently works with the copy should follow it and be informed when any style changes occur.

HOW TO BEGIN

Start listing points on your style sheet during the second reading, not the first. The reasons: If your first pass is one of comparison reading, it will be too disruptive to you (and to the copyholder) if you must stop to make periodic style sheet entries at the same time you are comparing dead and live copy. Also, once you have read the copy, you will have a clearer understanding of the content. This makes it easier to determine what the style point is or what it should be.

As you read, begin writing down each point, as you come to it, in the appropriate section. Try to remember (from the first reading) whether that point is repeated in the manuscript. Even if you don't remember whether it recurs in the text, write it down on the style sheet if it looks as though it might be useful later.

If a different usage of the same point appears in the text and there is no previously determined style, make (or seek) a decision on style treatment before you read further. You don't want to have to search through the entire document to find and change them all. An alternative style might be acceptable. Use the same style—or an approved alternative—for all similar points.

For the sake of speed, this style sheet need not be typed, especially if it will be used only by you for a single manuscript. But if the same subject and style will be used in subsequent assignments, and especially if the style sheet will be followed by co-workers, an eventual typing and alphabetizing of the guide will make it easier for everyone to use.

Client Style Sheet

In advertising agencies, client style sheets are compiled in a similar fashion, except there most likely will be a few pre-existing rules from the client before copy writing, or even conception, actually begins. (See Appendix G for an example of a client style sheet.)

A style sheet for client copy is referred to repeatedly by writers, typists, and proofreaders. Once style has been established, it should be typed and distributed to office personnel who work with the client. A copy should also be given to the client for information and approval. Separate style sheets are maintained for each client. They are minutely detailed, as are manuscript style sheets.

An agency usually has many different clients. Those clients have products with different "personalities." And so will the ads created for them. Copy language may be formal and businesslike for a bank client, casual and playful for a client who owns a pizza shop. Typeface and layout design will be chosen accordingly by the art director.

Clients may have additional copy style preferences. One client may use a comma between its corporate name and the word "Inc." Another client may not. One may capitalize, or even spell, certain keywords in ways not ordinarily recognized by a dictionary. Some clients may want a registration mark after every mention of their product names; others may require only one registration mark per page. Some may want copyright lines and other legal footnotes at the bottom of their ads; others may not. Trade names used as possessives are not allowed by many clients; product names used as adjectives or as nouns may also be forbidden. Client preferences are often too numerous to remember and always too important to forget. So keep a list of them.

HOW TO BEGIN

Client style and product information emanate from the client to the account executive, who passes it along to the copywriter. The copywriter, the art director, and occasionally the creative director will create the ad.

The proofreader is the custodian of the original style sheet, compiling it while proofreading the ad copy. You should make sure that the style sheet reflects the exact style designed by the creative team, that everyone on the team always has an up-to-date version of it, and that it is followed precisely in each advertisement. When style deviations or changes occur, the proofreader will consult with the writer or account executive for a decision, then notify all others involved with the client account of subsequent changes in style.

Most client style sheets evolve as an ad campaign progresses. There will likely be additions, deletions, and changes in style during the next ad campaign. Keeping the style sheet current and enforcing the rules are among the hardest and most important challenges of the proofreader. One deviation could lead to another, and the style would become a useless collection of contradictory rules. Inconsistency can destroy otherwise good ad copy, not to mention friendly client-agency relationships.

FIVE

Understanding the Writer's Language and Querying Effectively

The writer's craft is the proofreader's as well. And the most valuable resource a writer can have is a proofreader who knows the language and the mechanics that make it work.

There is a certain flexibility or permissiveness unique to the American English language. We often make one word where there used to be two; we change nouns to verbs and adjectives to nouns. We alter the meanings, even create new words when the old ones seem inadequate.

STUDY IT

A word can be misused for such a long time that its correct usage begins to sound awkward. Meanwhile, some dictionaries—at least those with a penchant for bending established order to accommodate popular usage—have made its misuses officially acceptable.

The question then raised is, Whose rules are we to follow? The purist can become hopelessly entangled in and frustrated by conflicting viewpoints of language experts, and the result can be a total inability to make any firm commitment. Indecision can break the best of proofreaders. But so can rigidity.

Efforts to resolve this issue concerning the language have been documented as far back as 200 years. James Adams's idea of "refining, correcting, improving, and ascertaining the English language" was squelched by Thomas Jefferson: ". . . Judicious neology [the coining of a new word, phrase, or expression from conversation] can alone give strength and copiousness to language, and enable it to be the vehicle of new ideas," reflected Mr. Jefferson. There is no recorded resolution.

The war over words continues even today between the progressive and the dogmatic. Usage Notes in *The American Heritage Dictionary of the English Language,* third edition, track problem words from past to present-day usage. The accompanying observations and varying opinions of a Usage Panel—a collection of 173 well-known writers, critics, and scholars—present an arsenal of viewpoints from which the reader can make an informed decision.

Our language continues to grow, changing faster than any other language in the world, and the proofreader must keep pace by developing an extraordinary curiosity and sensitivity to the transition.

If reading is one of your major means of outside entertainment (as it is for many proofreaders), you will find it a source for many new words to add to your vocabulary. Study "Words and Phrases Commonly Confused or Misused" (Appendix D). Or create your own list of potential troublemakers and keep them close by.

A good dictionary is the most valuable resource a proofreader can have. There is a wealth of information therein that few people ever bother to consider—or even know is included! Learn how to use it by studying the guides and explanatory notes in the front matter. There you will find the key to word meanings and pronunciations and to words or expressions unique to a specific region or unacceptable (nonstandard) everywhere. You will also learn how to find idioms, colloquialisms, parts of speech, verb tenses, antonyms, homonyms, abbreviations, even examples of sentences in which the word is used. Signs, symbols, measurement tables, geographic and biographical entries, proofreading symbols—the list goes on. A good dictionary is the proofreader's best friend. Keep your dictionary close by whenever and wherever you read.

There will always be dictionaries and other reference books that accept what you might consider a suspect word or definition faster than you do. If it is sanctioned by a reputable source, the writer has a justifiable claim to it. If it is not approved on good authority, it is a point of concern and should be flagged by the proofreader.

A simpler solution is to require office staff to use a specific standard. For example, McGraw-Hill asks that its writers, editors, and proofreaders conform as closely as possible to the current edition of *Merriam-Webster's Collegiate Dictionary* and, for further reference, to the current edition of *The Chicago Manual of Style*.

The conversational word and the written word also have recognized differences. Written copy is more formal; the language should not be corrupted, as it frequently—and unfortunately—is in dialogue.

S-P-E-L-L IT RIGHT

Good spellers are usually born, not made. If learning to spell comes hard, so will recognizing a misspelled word. Certain words will stump the best of spellers. And if you can't remember them, it's not a blemish on your reputation if you have to look them up and store them in your style sheet for future reference.

The spell-checker in word processing programs should eliminate most of the misspellings before the proofreader sees the copy, but it won't catch everything. It won't catch a word that is spelled correctly but used incorrectly. It also cannot distinguish between a right word and a wrong word if both are spelled correctly. If "discreet" was typed when "discrete" was meant, the computer won't find an error, but a proofreader who understands context—and knows how to spell—will.

Incorrect word breaks are another mistake a good proofreader just doesn't allow to happen. Words that are spelled the same but have two different meanings or grammatical usages may also be divided differently (for example, *pre-sent* (verb) and *pres-ent* (adjective and noun)). Learn the rules for determining syllables, and when in doubt, look it up.

How do you find a word in the dictionary if you can't spell it? Look it up the way it sounds. If you can't find it there, try another combination of letters with the same sound. Learning how a word is pronounced may also help you spell it correctly.

When looking up words, read the entire definition. Some words have variant meanings and pronunciations, as well as different spellings and syllable breaks. Either variant may be acceptable, or there may be an official preference. British spellings, often side by side with American spellings in a dictionary, should not be used in the United States.

PARLEZ-VOUS . . . ?

Unless you are fluent in a foreign language, proofreading it, even in occasional phrases, can be tricky. A Spanish word can convey one meaning to a Miami reader, a different meaning to a reader in Texas. Proofreaders who don't know the language well should not look for anything other than typographical errors.

KNOW THE MECHANICS

Extraordinary as it may seem, many writers do not know, much less use correctly, the tools of their own trade. Grammar and punctuation make the language work, and the proofreader's knowledge of both is vital. For most people, formal study of the mechanics doesn't extend beyond high school. If memories of it are dim, take a refresher course or dig out your old textbook (or your dictionary), study it, and refer to it as often as you need to. You may be the only grammatical lifeline between the typed copy and the published word.

There are many good grammar and punctuation books on the market, in both college and commercial bookstores. Although the content in all of them is mostly the same, examine each before you buy and choose one that is easy to read, clear in explanation, and thorough.

WHEN TO QUERY

Don't be afraid to ask questions. If something about the copy looks wrong, query it. (See Table 5.1 for points of query.) You should never be embarrassed about asking questions. You may learn from them. It is those questions you don't ask that can come back to haunt you. Querying decisively means asking questions but using good judgment at the same time.

Good writing deserves good proofreading; bad writing demands it. More often than writers like to admit, they make errors—of grammar, punctuation, spelling, awkward phrasing, even facts. A good proofreader feels accountable for every one of these errors.

Just how much responsibility should you as a proofreader try to assume? Short of rewriting the copy and making needless changes, just as much as you are capable of. It is your duty to catch, or at least query, everything you think is wrong, no matter whose formal responsibility it may be. But you must be as informed as you can be of the point in question and approach with great caution any error that is outside your assigned duties.

There is sometimes a thin line between proofreading and copyediting. Make sure you know the difference. Correcting copy is the proofreader's job. Changing copy is the editor's (or writer's).

TABLE 5.1

Points of Query

Subject and verb agreement
Incorrect grammar or word usage
Punctuation inconsistency
Factual inaccuracy or inconsistency
Contradiction or repetition
Clarity or meaning

WHAT TO QUERY

Proofreaders shouldn't extend their questions into what is the editor's or writer's domain, such as badly written sentences. If you think a sentence needs a closer look, you should point out something wrong (such as a comma splice or a dangling phrase) or confusing (such as a change of tense).

Don't ask idle questions about problems you haven't researched. While you will learn plenty on the job, most of what you learn should result from your own study and observation; neither the editor nor the writer has the time (or probably the inclination) to teach you. Whatever you query, do it carefully and thoughtfully.

Correcting mistakes or querying what you believe is an error always calls for diplomacy and, in some instances, persuasive strategy. If it was obvious that the writer didn't know better, cite or attach rules from authoritative sources. This says to the writer that you gave intelligent thought to the problem and that you didn't make up the rule (you will often be challenged if you don't). While this helps the writer understand and learn from mistakes, it also helps the writer decide whether to bend or break the rules.

If a rule is intentionally broken or if the writer disagrees with one of your suggestions, you need to understand why. Discuss it when you both have the opportunity. You may learn something. To correct or not is the writer's (or editor's) choice. And even if you think it is the wrong choice, you must learn to live with that particular limitation of the proofreader's job.

Some writers are resistant to any suggestions, and the proofreader must learn to live with that, as well. Under all circumstances, remember that the proofreader is the writer's ally and support, not competition. Building trust between yourself and the writer is essential to the success of an assignment, as well as to your own success as an effective (and employed) proofreader.

HOW TO QUERY

The easiest way to query is to circle or highlight the word or words in question. In the margin or on a Post-it® note, write a question mark and circle it, or write out *okay?* and circle it. (The circled mark in the margin indicates only an instruction or question; if you don't circle it, this implies that you want the mark typed or typeset.)

The circled query mark, alone in the margin, can place a burden on the editor or writer, who must try to guess why the word or words caused you concern. What confused *you* may not be as quickly evident to *them*. You'll get better results if you write out your question.

If your query is ignored, it may have been overlooked or not understood. Restate your question and send it back to the person who can answer the question. Write out what problem you think the word has created or the rule that you think may have been broken. This gives the writer full information and a choice of solving the problem or leaving the copy as it is.

Another way to ask questions is to make a query list as you read, noting the page number and line reference, and writing down the specific questions you may have. The separate query list (or, with the list in hand, a conversation with the writer or editor) is often the only method available to you when you are correcting copy at a computer workstation. Writing down your questions is also a good way to query when you are reading long copy. Answers to questions you initially may have could become evident as you get further into the copy, and a query won't be necessary by the time you reach the end of the job.

If you proofread in a situation where the writer or editor is not present (such as for a printer), you must handle corrections and queries differently than proofreaders in editorial or other business offices. And your company's policy is usually firm: Do not change the customer's copy. If it is a simple spelling or grammati-

cal error—and you must be absolutely sure that it is an error—
make the change (but always with a notation to the customer).
Don't get too involved with customer copy except, of course, to
correct the typesetter's mistakes. It is time-consuming, it is beyond
your area of responsibility, and it could alienate the customer.

SIX

Giving Clear Instructions

PROOFREADER'S MARKS

Proofreader's marks are shorthand symbols that everyone in the trade understands and uses. (See the comprehensive list in Table 6.1.) While they may look like a foreign language, close study will reveal logic and simplicity. One proof mark will often substitute for many words and be recognized instantly by anyone working with the copy.

Although most symbols are standard throughout the communications industry, you will discover a few variations from office to office if you are in the business long enough. You may want to adapt to them or request that your co-workers conform to yours. Either way, standardizing the marks office-wide avoids confusion. The main objective is getting the message across clearly and quickly.

Proofreader's marks are a vital communication link among the members of the creative team. They also transmit the same important information to the typesetter and printer.

HOW TO MAKE THE MARKS

Copy corrections must be conveyed as neatly and concisely as possible. Use an indelible-ink pen or a colored pencil on a manuscript or a reader's proof (both of which are typically laser prints); the color red is easiest to see. Use a nonreproducing pen (usually light blue) on camera-ready copy and an indelible-ink pen on a printer's proof. There are several reasons why a lead pencil should

Text continues on page 58.

TABLE 6.1

Proofreader's Marks

Explanation	Mark in margin	Mark in copy	Corrected copy
delete character	℘	the careful /reader	the careful reader
delete word	℘	the ~~careful~~ reader	the reader
close up space	‿	the careful r‿eader	the careful reader
delete and close up space	℘̃	the careful r⌿eader	the careful reader
lowercase letter	(lc)	⟋The careful reader	the careful reader
lowercase letters	(lc)/③	⟋The ¢areful ⟋Reader	the careful reader
lowercase word	(lc)	⟋THE careful reader	the careful reader
ruled line, underscore	(rule)	the <u>careful</u> reader	the careful reader
	(us)	the <u>careful</u> reader	the <u>careful</u> reader
italic type	(ital)	the careful reader	the *careful* reader
roman type	(rom)	the (careful) reader	the careful reader
lightface type	(lf)	the (careful) reader	the careful reader
boldface type	(bf)	the careful reader	the **careful** reader
boldface italic type	(bf ital)	the careful reader	the ***careful*** reader
small capital letters	(sc)	The Careful Reader	THE CAREFUL READER
	(sm cap)	The Careful Reader	THE CAREFUL READER
capital letter	(cap)	the careful reader	The careful reader
capital words	(cap)	the careful reader	THE CAREFUL READER
capitalize and italicize	(cap ital)	the careful reader	*THE CAREFUL READER*
subscript	⌄2	H₂O	H_2O
superscript	⌃2	the careful reader²	the careful reader^2
transpose characters	(tr)	the craeful reader	the careful reader
transpose words	(tr)	the reader careful	the careful reader

TABLE 6.1 (continued)

Explanation	Mark in margin	Mark in copy	Corrected copy
let it stand; disregard previous correction	(stet)	the ~~careful~~ reader	the careful reader
words missing; see original copy	(OSC)	The‸to what is being read.	The careful reader pays close attention to what is being read.
spell out	(sp)	②careful readers	two careful readers
ligature	ﬁ	ﬁnally, a careful reader	finally, a careful reader
	(lig)	ﬁnally, a careful reader	finally, a careful reader
diphthong	o͡e	Caesar's œuvre	Caesar's œuvre
	(diph)	Caesar's œuvre	Caesar's œuvre
query	(careful?)	Are you a‸reader?	Are you a careful reader?
	careful⑦	Are you a‸reader?	Are you a careful reader?
	careful(OK?)	Are you a‸reader?	Are you a careful reader?
insert space	#	the‸careful reader	the careful reader
Insert period	⊙	The careful reader‸	The careful reader.
insert comma	⋏	the careful‸attentive reader	the careful, attentive reader
insert semicolon	⋏;	the careful reader‸the thoughtful reader	the careful reader; the thoughtful reader
insert colon	(:)	the careful reader‸	the careful reader:
insert apostrophe	ᵛ	the careful readerˇs guide	the careful reader's guide
Insert quotation marks	ᵛ/ᵛ	ˇthe careful readerᵛ	"the careful reader"
insert character	a	the cᵡeful reader	the careful reader
insert word	careful	the‸reader	the careful reader
insert asterisk	✳	the carefulˇreader	the careful* reader
insert dagger	†	the careful reader‸	the careful reader†
	(set dagger)	the careful reader‸	the careful reader†

Continued.

TABLE 6.1 **Proofreader's Marks** (continued)

Explanation	Mark in margin	Mark in copy	Corrected copy
insert double dagger	‡	the careful reader∧	the careful reader‡
	(set dbl dag)	the careful reader∧	the careful reader‡
insert slash (virgule)	⧸	the careful reader∧	the careful reader/
	(set slash)	the careful reader∧	the careful reader/
insert parentheses	{ / }	the∧careful∧reader	the (careful) reader
insert brackets	⟦ / ⟧	the∧careful∧reader	the [careful] reader
en dash	$\frac{1}{N}$	1948-1955	1948–1955
1-em dash	$\frac{1}{M}$	Reading carefully--not something everyone can do.	Reading carefully—not something everyone can do.
hyphen	=/=	Read word∧for∧word.	Read word-for-word.
invert	↺	(the careful reader)	the careful reader
indent 1 em	☐	]the careful reader	the careful reader
indent 2 ems	2	]the careful reader	the careful reader
	☐☐	]the careful reader	the careful reader
begin paragraph	¶	Do you know any careful readers? We need one as soon as possible.	Do you know any careful readers? We need one as soon as possible.
no paragraph; run in	‿	Do you know any careful readers? We need one.	Do you know any careful readers? We need one.
	(run in)	Do you know any careful readers? We need one.	Do you know any careful readers? We need one.
align	‖	‖the careful reader	the careful reader
	(align)	‖the careful reader	the careful reader

TABLE 6.1 (continued)

Explanation	Mark in margin	Mark in copy	Corrected copy
straighten line	=	the <u>careful</u> reader	the careful reader
move down	⊔	the cᵃreful reader	the careful reader
move up	⊓	the c₍a₎reful reader	the careful reader
move left	[	[the careful reader	the careful reader
	(fl)	[the careful reader	the careful reader
move right	]	] the careful reader	the careful reader
	(fr)	] the careful reader	the careful reader
center	] [	] the careful reader [	the careful reader
open type	(open)	the caไeful reader	the careful reader
close type	(close)	the carˡeful reader	the careful reader
	(kern)	the carˡeful reader	the careful reader
fix hole	(bad rag)	Reading carefully is something not ◯ everyone can do.	Reading carefully is something not every-one can do.
equal spacing	(eq #)	the ₍ₓ₎careful ₍ₓ₎reader	the careful reader
begin new line	⌐	Reading carefully is something not⌐every person can do,	Reading carefully is something not every person can do.
bad break	(BB)	Reading carefully is not something (ever-) yone can do.	Reading carefully is not something every-one can do.
	ev-ery-one	Reading carefully is not something (ever-) yone can do.	Reading carefully is not something every-one can do.
wrong font	(wf)	the careful (reader)	the careful reader
broken type/dirty proof	X	the carefu̷l reader	the careful reader
widow (also two-letter break)	(widow)	The careful read-er.	The careful reader.

not be used: Lead marks are indistinct and will fade over time. Corrections can easily be overlooked. Lead-pencil corrections can be erased. Make sure you have permanent proof of your work.

Be consistent, clear, and neat. Remember, these marks are your signature.

WHERE THE MARKS GO

- The proofreader should indicate inside the copy where the change is to be made.
- The instructive proof mark, the one indicating what the change is, is made in the margin.
- Every in-text mark must correspond to a marginal mark.

Some proofreaders yield to the temptation to omit the marginal mark and write instructions directly inside the copy. And there is sometimes good argument for doing so, especially if there is insufficient marginal space but ample space between the characters, words, and lines of type. This is not recommended for a variety of reasons. An in-text correction, with no marginal mark, is much more likely to be missed than a marginal correction that instantly flags the line where the correction is to be made and indicates what the correction should be. In-text instructions by the proofreader can also interfere with the editor's in-text marks, if there are any. So if you are tempted to make your instructions in the text, weigh the disadvantages first.

When instructions are made in the margin, use only one margin, not both, for each column of type. If there is more than one column of type on the page, proof marks for all columns should be systematically either on their left or their right—and not on the right margin for one and the left margin for another (unless there are only two columns of type on the page and the margin between them is narrow).

Because there may be more than one correction on a line, begin making proof marks at the far left side of the margin, separate individual changes with a slash, and work toward the right. Make sure your instructions are positioned directly across from the line being corrected.

Overcrowding sometimes occurs in one margin, and some proofreaders will make corrections in both margins, using whichever margin is closer to the error. The problems this creates outweigh any real justification for using this method. The corrections will not be in order, and jumping from one margin to another, then back to the text in search of the error, can often cause confusion for the typesetter or whoever will read the copy next. Avoid this procedure if at all possible.

In the following section, the marks to be made inside the text are in *italics,* the marginal marks in **boldface**. *Boldface and italicized* marks indicate they are used both inside the text and in the margin. As you read this section, refer to Table 6.1 as a visual guide.

WHAT THE MARKS MEAN

The *circle* is used inside the text around a word that is to be reset in another font or face or around numbers that are to be spelled out. In the margin, **circle** the instruction. Don't circle words that are to be typed or typeset. Broken type or dirty proof is circled in the text, but the corresponding marginal mark, **X**, is not circled because it could be mistaken for the now-obsolete symbol for a period. (Broken type or dirty proof may be found on camera-ready copy or a printer's proof, and it is marked in the text to alert the typesetter to check and correct it. Such type is not typically found on laser prints, whether of manuscript or typeset copy.)

The circle is also used in the text to indicate a bad rag, which is a hole of space at the beginnings or ends of lines of copy created by erratic line breaks. Make a circle inside the hole, then in the margin write **bad rag** or **hole** or **fix rag** (circled). To assist the typesetter in correcting a bad rag, see "Margin Rag" on page 110. A bad word break is also marked with a circle. In the margin write

BB (circled) or write out the word, showing all acceptable word breaks (don't circle).

The circle is used in text for words that the proofreader may question for some reason. The marginal query mark, **?**, should also be circled, or the typist or typesetter will set a question mark. Also circle in text any unusual word that might be questioned by the typist or typesetter, and in the margin write **ok** or **sic** or **cq** (circled) to indicate the unusual but correct spelling. The period can be easily lost in the margin and should be circled: **.** (circled). So should the colon: **:** (circled). The space symbol, **#**, should also be circled to avoid confusion with the symbol for pound or number (which is not circled).

The following marginal instructions should also be circled:

stet	let it stand
lc	lowercase
cap	capitalize
clc	capitalize and lowercase
sc	small capital letters
rom	roman type
ital	italic type
bf	boldface type
lf	lightface type
wf	wrong font
tr	transpose
sp	spell it out
fig	set in figures (numerals)
fl	flush left lines or margins
fr	flush right lines or margins
run in	delete a paragraph indent
DNS	do not set
TK	additional copy to come
PE	printer's error
EA	editor's alteration

In-text instructions for these marks follow.

The **dele** sign, pronounced "dee-lee," is a marginal correction meaning to delete. It is rarely drawn properly and is often mistaken for an "e." Practice drawing it correctly. The dele should not be used alone unless an empty space is intended or unless the result is obvious. Be cautious when using it alone, for what may look clear to you may not look that way to the typesetter. For example, you want to give instructions to delete the hyphen in the word "by-pass." If you use the dele sign alone and if the instruction is followed precisely, the result is "by pass" when you may have intended "bypass." Deletion of a hyphen at the end of a line of type may also create the same kind of confusion unless additional instructions, such as a close-up sign, are given.

A *close-up sign* should accompany the dele sign to indicate "bypass." It is used to close up space between characters and words and is drawn both in the text and the margin. If it is drawn carelessly, the result may be the closing up of unintended characters or words. The sign is not used to close up tiny spaces between characters and words or to close up widely spaced lines of type (see the discussion on word spacing and letterspacing on pages 99–102).

The *top part of the close-up sign* is used in the text and in the margin to indicate a ligature, the joining of two letters (fi becomes fi). It is also used for the diphthong (oe becomes œ). The respective marginal marks for these are **lig** and **diph** (circled).

A *caret* in the text should be used to flag the insertion of a word and most punctuation marks. Draw the caret at the bottom of the line where the insertion is to be made. A corresponding caret is used in the margin to umbrella these marks: the **comma**, the **semicolon**, and the **subscript**. A marginal caret over a letter, word, or numeral insertion is not necessary.

An *inverted caret* goes inside the text to indicate the following insertions, and again under the insertions in the margin: **apostrophe**, **quotation marks**, **superscript**, and **asterisk**. Inside the text, draw the inverted caret at the top of the line where the insertion is to be made.

The *slash, slant,* or *virgule* has many uses and is also a type character. It is used in the text to indicate lowercase. CAPITAL with a *slash* through the C and a *horizontal line* over the letters that follow becomes capital. CAPITAL with a *slash* through the A and a *horizontal line* over the letters that follow becomes Capital. Marginal marks are circled **lc** and **clc** (or **ulc** for upper- and lowercase), respectively.

When there is more than one correction on a line of type, the **slash** (or **slant**) is also used in the margin to separate each marginal instruction.

If two identical changes occur consecutively on the same line of copy, it isn't necessary to repeat the change in the margin. Make the marginal instruction once, then follow with two slashes instead of one. If more than three identical changes occur consecutively, make one slash, then follow with the number of times the change occurs. Circle the number.

If a slash is to be typed or typeset as part of the copy, place a *caret* in the text at the appropriate place; the marginal mark is a **slash** (not circled) or a **slash with two horizontal lines across it**, or write the words **set slash** (circled) in the margin.

A *vertical line* through a character inside the copy indicates a change or deletion; between two characters it can be used instead of a caret to indicate the insertion of a space or an additional character(s). The vertical line must be accompanied by marginal instructions. Words or characters to be substituted or added in the text are written in the margin and are not circled. Remember, the marginal space mark is # (circled).

Two vertical lines in the margin and text indicate that a line of type should be horizontally aligned with the other lines. A *right bracket* or a *left bracket* may also be used to indicate flush left or flush right lines or margins. A set of *brackets* facing away from each other is the instruction to center the copy. If the brackets face each other, the copy is to be justified.

A *horizontal line* is drawn through an entire word if it is to be changed or deleted. If the word is to be replaced by another word, write out the new word in the margin, but don't circle it. The dele sign is not necessary. If a word is to be deleted entirely, the marginal mark is the **dele** sign. This is one instance where the dele sign is not accompanied by the close-up sign, as it would specify that you want the adjoining words connected.

A *horizontal line* is drawn directly under a word or words that you want italicized. The marginal instruction is **ital** (circled). If a rule (underscore) is intended, draw the horizontal line under the word(s), then write **rule** or **us** (circled) in the margin. For typeset copy, you must also indicate in the margin the weight of the rule (see the discussion on ruled lines on page 94).

A *wavy horizontal line* under a letter or word instructs the typist or typesetter to make it boldface. The marginal mark is **bf** (circled).

When a word must be boldface and italic, underscore with both a *horizontal line* and a *wavy line,* then write and circle **bf ital** in the margin.

Two horizontal lines under a letter or word indicate that small capital letters are to be set. The marginal mark is **sc** (circled). *Three horizontal lines* are used for capital letters, and the marginal mark is **cap** (circled). And *four horizontal lines* are instructions for capital italicized letters or words. The marginal mark is **cap ital** (circled).

Two horizontal lines, one above and one below a word or line of type, mean that vertical alignment is needed. The word **align** (circled) or two **horizontal lines** (not circled) are the marginal marks.

A *horizontal bracket* in the text and in the margin is the instruction to move a character, word, or line up or down.

A *paragraph symbol* is used as an in-text instruction to begin a new paragraph. If it isn't drawn carefully, it can be confused with the space symbol **#**. Another mark used for a new paragraph is an *L-shaped symbol.* Make corresponding symbols for marginal instructions and circle them. More common in typeset copy is the use of an **open box** in the margin, with a number inside to indicate the precise measurement of the indent in em spaces. For example, an **empty open box** is the symbol for a one-em space or indent, a **box with the numeral 2** inside for a two-em space or indent, and so on. An **open box with a diagonal from the lower left to upper right corners** is the symbol for a one-en space or indent. (See also "Em and En Spaces" on page 102.)

A *curved line* (in the shape of a reversed S) in text is the instruction to run in one line of copy with another line, such as joining a sentence to a paragraph above it. If the end of the sentence is some distance from the beginning of the paragraph, *two shorter curved lines* may also be used symbolically to join the two. The marginal instruction is **run in** (circled).

Three check marks or **eq #** (circled) in the margin tells the typesetter that characters or words are unevenly spaced. A *check mark* or *caret* at the space between characters or words in the text indicates the place(s) affected.

A *small vertical line* can also be used between typeset characters or words where there is too much space. The circled marginal instruction is **close**. A *small plus sign* in the text is used between occasional word or character groupings to point out that spacing is too tight. The circled marginal instruction is **open**. (See the discussion on word spacing and letterspacing on pages 99–102.) If all characters or words on a page are too tightly or loosely spaced in typeset copy, write and circle **open type** or **close type** at the top of the page. Make sure you have double-checked the instructions (type specifications) to the typesetter before making your decisions. The odd spacing could be intentional. These instructions are used only in typeset copy.

A *horizontal S-curve* around characters or words inside the text is used to transpose them. The marginal instruction for transpose is **tr** (circled). If the copy type is so small that characters or words may be obscured by the horizontal S-curve, circle them, then write **tr** (circled) in the margin. If the transposition is complicated or likely to be misunderstood, circle all of the affected words and write them out correctly in the margin. Sentences may be transposed by numbering them, in the text, in the order in which they should appear, then writing **tr** (circled) in the margin.

The word **stet** is Latin for *let it stand*. It is written and circled **stet** in the margin to void a previous proofreading correction or change. In the text, place *dots* under the character(s) or word(s) affected.

Out, See Copy or **OSC** (circled) is a marginal note that some words in the dead copy have been omitted from the live copy. A *caret* is used in the live copy text to mark the spot where the omission begins. So that the typesetter will not have to search through the dead copy for the missing words, also mark the area in the dead copy with *carets* (where the omission begins and ends), then write **OSC** (circled) in the margin of the dead copy. Avoid using **sc** (circled) for "see copy," as this is the instruction for small capital letters. If only a word or a few words are missing from the live copy—and if there is enough room to do so—write them in the margin and spare the typesetter the trouble of searching through the dead copy.

The **invert sign** is used when a character or word or line of type has been printed upside down. Unlikely to happen in computerized typography, this can occur in handset metal typesetting or in careless paste-up of typeset copy. Circle the affected character(s), then use the invert sign as a marginal mark.

Other symbols are used for letters or numerals that have similar shapes and could be misinterpreted by the typist or the typesetter:

o	the letter o
Ø	the numeral 0
2	the numeral 2
ƶ	the letter z
1	the numeral 1
⁊	the numeral 7
ⓔⓛ	the lowercase l

Sometimes there is no symbol or straightforward means to instruct the typesetter, especially for mathematical, scientific, or technical terms, or for reference marks such as the dagger or asterisk, ampersand, and bullet. Write out the instruction.

Don't invent new proof marks. They will confuse the person reading the corrections, and later even you may not recognize them or what they stand for.

Table 6.2 shows the original copy and Table 6.3 shows the proofreader's marks to correct the new copy.

TABLE 6.2

Original (Dead) Copy

Proofreading for Perfect Copy

Proofreading is a step-by-step procedure that must be followed carefully.

First you will compare the original (dead) copy against the newly typed or typeset (live) copy. You will either comparison read alone, with a copyholder, or with the aid of a tape recorder. After comparison reading, read the live copy again as many times as necessary to find and correct all the errors. When there is no dead copy to compare the live copy against, you will read the live copy alone. This procedure is called noncomparison reading.

A proofreader is responsible not only for typographical and spelling errors, copy omissions, and format, but often for style, word usage, grammar, and punctuation as well. Some of these duties may require more editorial or academic training than some proofreaders may have, but you should give as much back-up support as you are qualified, and allowed, to do.

Read slowly. Read carefully. Research before you query. And remember, all corrections you make, or changes you suggest, must be approved by the writer or editor before they are included.

The proofreader has additional duties if the copy is then typeset. The reader's proof, as this typeset copy is called, should be read for typographical errors and deviations from the original (dead) copy. These proofs are also read by the writer and the editor. Make sure that their changes--and your corrections--are combined on one proof before it is sent to the typesetter for revisions. When revisions are made, read the revised proof as thoroughly as you read the first proof. *New* errors can occur as the *old* ones are corrected, so **keep your eyes open!**

TABLE 6.3

New (Live) Copy with Proofreader's Marks

Marks	Text
] [=/=	] **Proofreading for Perfect Copy** [Proofreading is a step‿by‿step procedure that must be followed carefully.
②/will	] First you‿compare the original (dead) copy against the newly typed or typeset (live)
⊙	copy‿You will either comparison read alone, with a copyholder, or with the aid of a tape recorder. After comparison reading, read the
﹖	live copy again as many ~~many~~ times as necessary to find and correct all the errors.
ϑ̃	When there is no d¢ead copy to compare the live copy against, you will read the live
(hole)	copy alone. This procedure is called ◯ noncomparison reading.
(stet)	A proofreader is responsible ~~not only~~ for typographical and spelling errors, copy omissions, and format, but often for style, word usage, grammar, and punctuation as well. Some of these duties may require
(lc)/③	more ℰditorial or ⋀cademic ⊤raining than some proofreaders may have, but you should give as much back-up support as you are qualified, and allowed, to do.
(tr)	[Read carefully.]Read slowly.]Research be⁀fore you query. ͺ
(run in)	⌐And remember, all corrections you make, or changes you suggest, must be approved by the writer or editor before they
(¶)	are included.[The proofreader has additional duties if the copy is then typeset. The
ᵛ/⋀	reader's proof‿as this typeset copy is called, should be read for typo⁀graphical errors and deviations from the original (dead) copy. These proofs are also read by the writer and
their / ¹/M ¹/M	the editor. Make sure that ~~there~~ changes⊝ and your corrections⊝are combined on one proof before it is sent to the typesetter for revisions. When revisions are made, read the revised proof as thoroughly as you read
(ital) (bf)/(BB) (widow)	the first proof. *New* errors can occur as the (old) ones are corrected, so keep your eyes (op‿ en!

COPY EDITOR'S MARKS

The proofreader's and the copy editor's marks are similar. The major difference is how they are used. The proofreader's marks are both at the point of trouble in text and in the margin. Copy-editing instructions are in text, and each mark is explicit and self-explanatory. Many of the copy editor's marks are simply a logical combination of what the proofreader uses both in text and in the margin. In fact, editors who work with single-spaced copy may use the proofreader's method of in-text flags and marginal corrections, or sometimes a combination of both methods. If you know the proofreader's marks, you will have no trouble recognizing and understanding the copy editor's marks.

When editing is done on hard copy before the copy is typed or keyed in a word processing file (rather than performed directly on an electronic file on-screen), the typist incorporates editorial changes while typing the original copy. As the copyediting marks are already inside the text, the typist doesn't have to interrupt typing speed to look in the margin for instructions. If the copy is already keyed, formatted, and printed out before the editor makes changes, the editor either will use the proofreader's method to make changes or will mark instructions in text on the printout and place a **check mark** in the margin of the printout beside the lines where the changes were made. This will allow the typesetter to pick out only corrections rather than having to read through the entire text again. This copy will eventually become the dead copy that will be compared by the proofreader with the newly typed/typeset (live) copy.

Copy Editor's Marks in the Age of Computers

Now that most manuscripts are written, copyedited, and sent to the typesetter all in one revised electronic file, proofreaders may encounter a type of copy editor's mark that is new in the world of computers—the embedded type code.

For example, the copyeditor may insert a symbol such as "{A}" to indicate an A-head, "{BL}" to indicate a bulleted list, or "{FN}" or "{F}" to indicate a footnote. The typesetter (or his or her page layout program) will automatically know to set these elements as directed by the specs from the art director or designer. (See more about type specs in Chapter 7.) The main thing a proofreader needs to know about embedded type codes in text is that the codes themselves should not appear in the typeset pages, and they should serve as an indication to the proofreader what each element should look like. (Proofreaders will often have sample pages—rather than, or in addition to, written specs—to refer to.)

In addition, embedded codes may be used to indicate special characters within the text. For example, "{c}" may be used to indicate a copyright mark (©), two hyphens ("--") may mean em-dash (—), "{d}" may mean degree mark (°), and "{n til}" may call for a lowercase letter *n* with a tilde (ñ). Be aware that not all publishers and offices handle these the same way. If you will be dealing with special characters, you should receive a list of such characters and what they mean.

SEVEN

Working with Type

Typefaces are a part of our daily lives, impossible to escape whether we are reading a book or a billboard, a recipe or a road map, movie credits or magazines. And identifying them is a fascinating adventure.

Before the prevalence of computers, the number of typefaces in circulation was estimated at between 2,000 and 3,000. However, with the advent and subsequent widespread use of the personal computer came an avalanche of "homegrown" fonts. Suddenly, it seems, every graphic designer became a type designer, though not necessarily a good one.

Computer software today allows for seemingly endless variations of a font, featuring programs that virtually eliminate written type specifications. With the touch of a few keystrokes to change font, point size, tracking, and leading, the designer can now "wrap" the copy until it fits nicely on the page.

There are a hundred thousand or more digital fonts now on the market, including those that are personally customized and all variations permitted by present-day computer software. And the number is growing. Although software can make it easier to create fonts and fit copy, it can never replace the knowledge and skill required for the truly successful artistic endeavor of designing type.

Typefaces, each with distinctive characteristics, should have one common purpose: to make thoughts visible.

An interest in typeface design adds still another dimension— and considerably more enjoyment—to the proofreader's job. Expertise in type identification, especially of the classic typefaces and certainly of those you work with daily, contributes even more to your professional worth. Every proofreader should know at least what makes one typeface different from another. For it will be your job, if you work for a typesetter or printer, to determine if the copy was set in the right face.

TYPE CLASSIFICATION

Because of the variety of typefaces, an established order has been attempted over the years. But type classification, as this arrangement has been called, has long been a source of debate among typographers, and no precisely systematic or universally accepted order exists. To further confuse the beginning student of type, some faces belong to several of these classifications. Below is one attempt at classification that groups typefaces by stress (vertical or diagonal), stroke (thick or thin), and serif (or sans serif).

Serif

The letters of serif typefaces have serifs (little cross-strokes at the end of the main strokes) and varying contrast of thick and thin strokes.

OLD STYLE

The letters resemble Roman inscriptions, are wide, round, and open, with pointed serifs curving into the stroke, and gentle contrasts between light and heavy strokes.*

The five boxing wizards jump quickly.   ADOBE GARAMOND
The five boxing wizards jump quickly.   BEMBO
The five boxing wizards jump quickly.   GALLIARD

---

*Unless otherwise noted, all pangrams in this chapter are set in 12-point type.

TRANSITIONAL

The letters are basically old style but show some transition to modern type. Serifs are more perpendicular, and the difference between thick and thin strokes is more defined.

The five boxing wizards jump quickly. NEW CALEDONIA
The five boxing wizards jump quickly. TIMES NEW ROMAN
The five boxing wizards jump quickly. UTOPIA

MODERN

The letters are more mechanically perfect than old style and transitional, and their thick and thin strokes are more sharply defined. Serifs are straight, flat, and perpendicular to the strokes.

The five boxing wizards jump quickly. BODONI
The five boxing wizards jump quickly. LINOTYPE DIDOT
The five boxing wizards jump quickly. WALBAUM

Modern Serif

Because of their contemporary look, which contrasts so greatly with Roman type, some serif faces must be classified separately.

SQUARE

The letters are primarily uniform in stroke thickness, with heavy slab serifs and no bracketing.

The five boxing wizards jump quickly. GLYPHA
The five boxing wizards jump quickly. LUBALIN GRAPH
The five boxing wizards jump quickly. MEMPHIS

ROUND

The letters employ the rounded shape of Roman type and the serifs are round and heavy.

The five boxing wizards jump quickly.   AMERICAN TYPEWRITER

The five boxing wizards jump quickly.   CHELTENHAM
The five boxing wizards jump quickly.   SOUVENIR

INSCRIBED

The letters are basically sans serif but the stems and bases widen slightly, giving a slightly chiseled effect, which suggests a serif.

The five boxing wizards jump quickly.   ALBERTUS
The five boxing wizards jump quickly.   OPTIMA
The five boxing wizards jump quickly.   POPPL-LAUDATIO

Sans Serif

The letters have no serifs and very little contrast between thick and thin strokes. These typefaces are sometimes called gothic in the United States.

The five boxing wizards jump quickly.   FRUTIGER
The five boxing wizards jump quickly.   FUTURA
The five boxing wizards jump quickly.   MYRIAD

Script

The letters have no serifs and are designed to resemble calligraphy or handwriting.*

The five boxing wizards jump quickly.   CAFLISCH SCRIPT
The five boxing wizards jump quickly.   MISTRAL
The five boxing wizards jump quickly.   VIVALDI

---

*The pangrams in script typefaces are set in 16-point type.

Ornamental

The letters have fanciful designs and are used to catch attention or evoke a mood.

The five boxing wizards jump quickly. ARNOLD BOECKLIN

The five boxing wizards jump quickly. HOBO

The five boxing wizards jump quickly. PAPYRUS

Black Letter

The letters resemble hand-drawn letters once made by scribes. The vertical strokes and angles are heavy and broad, with delicate and ornamental hairlines. These typefaces are also called Old English, gothic (in Europe), and text letters (not to be confused with text type).

the five Boxing wizards jump quickly.

AMERICAN UNCIAL

The five boxing wizards jump quickly. FETTE FRAKTUR

The five boxing wizards jump quickly. ZAPF CHANCERY

TYPE CATEGORIES

For practical purposes, typefaces can be consolidated into two general categories, display and text, which cross almost all classifications of type.

Display Type

Most typefaces are display faces, appropriately named as they function to establish a particular mood or emotion. They catch the reader's attention. They are often the message, rather than the conveyor of one. Display type can be found in nearly all classifica-

tions of type. Designs range from stark, straight lines to fancy flour-
ishes, with many variations in between. Uncomfortable to read in
lengthy settings, display type is used in heads and brief messages,
such as advertisements containing a few lines of copy, invitations,
and announcements.

The five boxing wizards jump quickly.   GIDDYUP

The five boxing wizards jump quickly.   HUMANA SANS

The five boxing wizards jump quickly.
                                               IMPROV

The five boxing wizards jump quickly.   OXFORD

The five boxing wizards jump quickly.   RUSSELL SQUARE

Text Type

Only a handful of typefaces of the thousands available are the ones
we see and read most often. These text faces (also called book
faces) are generally from the serif classification. Their shapes,
strokes, and serifs are designed to link the letters into groups
(words), allowing the eyes to flow smoothly from one letter to the
next. A text face does not attract attention to itself and is therefore
easier to read. Text type is used for most books, magazine articles,
dictionaries, and long body copy appearing in advertisements.

The five boxing wizards jump quickly.   ADOBE CASLON

The five boxing wizards jump quickly.   BERKELEY OLD STYLE

The five boxing wizards jump quickly.   JANSON TEXT

TYPE NAMES

The names of typefaces are often copyrighted and owned by companies that have exclusive rights to their uses. Their designs, however, are much more difficult to protect. And because of the wide
public appeal of some typefaces, companies that do not own the
original license will create a similar (but not identical) typeface to

offer their customers. The resulting typefaces may look like a well-known typeface to the untrained eye, but have slight variances *and* different names. Helvetica is a popular typeface that has many imitators, such as Arial.

The five boxing wizards jump quickly.   HELVETICA
The five boxing wizards jump quickly.   ARIAL

When a specific typeface isn't available, substituting another typeface with similar characteristics is common practice among some typesetters and printers and is generally accepted by their customers as well, who often don't know or object to the difference. But a proofreader should be prepared to know what makes one typeface different from another. There will be many times during your proofreading career when you will be called on to identify typefaces. You will need to know where to look and how to find them.

Typography classes or lectures are rare except in art design schools or through sponsorship by organizations of printing professionals. Most proofreaders learn how to identify typefaces on the job or on their own. Learning the basics of type identification is not hard to do. Use a typeface book or font reference or examine the fonts that are on your computer. Start by comparing those typefaces you proofread most often with the corresponding faces in a typeface book. You will soon know the characteristics of those faces so well that you will be ready to tackle some new ones.

IDENTIFYING TYPE

The most common ways to identify a typeface are (1) to compare the elements of individual letters that have been typeset to those in a typeface book, and (2) to use a Web site that identifies a typeface from your description of it (search the Internet for "font identifier"). The size, the shape, and the position of these elements are the key. (See Table 7.1.)

TABLE 7.1

Elements of Typefaces

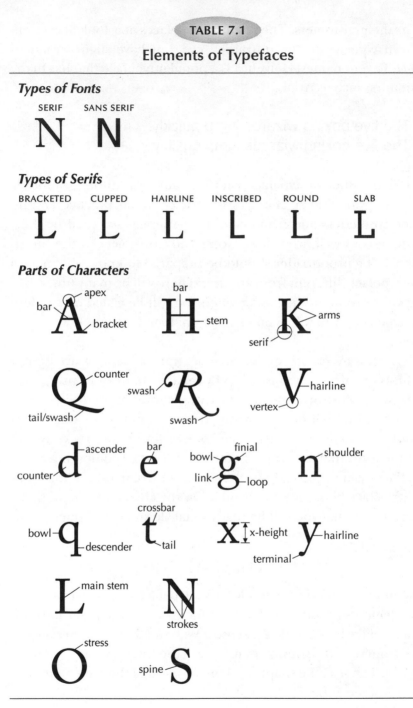

Types of Fonts

SERIF   SANS SERIF

Types of Serifs

BRACKETED   CUPPED   HAIRLINE   INSCRIBED   ROUND   SLAB

Parts of Characters

TABLE 7.1 (continued)

---

apex the inverted V-shape juncture of two stems, as in *A*

arm a horizontal or oblique stroke beginning at the main stem and ending free, as in *E* and *K*

ascender the part of the lowercase letters *b, d, f, h, i, j, k, l,* and *t* that extends above the x-line (see "The x-Height" on page 83)

bar the horizontal stroke in the *A, H, e,* and similar letters

bowl a curved stroke fully enclosing a counter, as in *g* and *q*

bracket the transition from the end of a serif to the stem, as in *q* and *A*

counter the fully or partially enclosed space within a letter, as in *O* and *Q*

crossbar a stroke cutting across a stem, as in *f* and *t*

descender the part of the letters *g, j, p, q,* and *y* that extends below the baseline

finial a small stroke projecting from the top of the *g;* also called an ear; also, any nonserif ending of a stroke

hairline the thin stroke of a letter, if there is one, as in *y* and *V*

link the stroke connecting the top and bottom of the *g*

loop the bottom part of a *g*

main stem the thicker stem of a letter, if there is one, as the long vertical strokes in *k* and *L*

serif a projection across the end of a stroke, as in *H*

shoulder the curved stroke of *h, m,* and *n*

spine the main curved stroke of an *s* or *S*

stem a vertical straight stroke (or the main oblique straight stroke if the letter has no vertical stroke), as the long strokes in *K* and *V*

stress the thickening of a curved stroke, as in *O*

stroke a straight or curved line necessary to form a letter, such as the three strokes in *N*

swash a flourish that replaces a terminal or serif, as in *ℛ*

tail the downward short stroke on *Q*

terminal the end of a stroke that doesn't end in a serif or finial, as in *y;* also called a kern

vertex the V-shaped juncture of two stems, as in *V*

x-height the height of lowercase letters, excluding ascenders and descenders

---

The Letters

Comparing individual letters in a typeface book is the way to begin. Start with the lowercase letter *g*, one of the most distinctive letters in any font.*

abcdefghijklmnopqrstuvwxyz	g	ADOBE CASLON
abcdefghijklmnopqrstuvwxyz	g	BODONI
abcdefghijklmnopqrstuvwxyz	**g**	CHELTENHAM
abcdefghijklmnopqrstuvwxyz	g	GOUDY OLD STYLE
abcdefghijklmnopqrstuvwxyz	g	PALATINO
abcdefghijklmnopqrstuvwxyz	g	WEISS

Using the *g* as a preliminary guide to typeface identification can eliminate many false leads. The elements of the *g* are the bowl, the loop, the link between the bowl and the loop, and the finial.

Once you think the typeset *g* has been identified as a match with one in the typeface book, go on to a few other letters in the book. Compare the capital letters *T, E, F, H,* and *A,* as well as the lowercase letters *t, e,* and *f.* The crossbars of these letters can be high, low, or centered, or long or short, and provide valuable clues to identification.

T E F H A t e f	ADOBE CASLON
T E F H A t e f	BODONI
T E F H A t e f	CHELTENHAM
T E F H A t e f	GOUDY OLD STYLE

---

*The alphabet series of these typefaces are set in 12-point type; the standalone *g*'s are set in 14-point type.

T E F H A t e f   PALATINO
T E F H A t e f   WEISS

The thickness of the strokes in the capital letters *L, N,* and *O* can also help you identify a particular typeface. Also, compare the shape and posture of the capital *O.* Then compare the height and shape of the bowls on the capital *P* or *R.*

L N O P R   ADOBE CASLON
L N O P R   BODONI
L N O P R   CHELTENHAM
L N O P R   GOUDY OLD STYLE
L N O P R   PALATINO
L N O P R   WEISS

Serif or Sans Serif

With their many different shapes, angles, and sizes, serifs give obvious identification clues. Examine the differences among the following typefaces.

abcdefghijklmnopqrstuvwxyz   ADOBE CASLON
ABCDEFGHIJKLMNOPQRSTUVWXYZ
1234567890.,;:"&!?$

abcdefghijklmnopqrstuvwxyz   BODONI
ABCDEFGHIJKLMNOPQRSTUVWXYZ
1234567890.,;:"&!?$

abcdefghijklmnopqrstuvwxyz   FUTURA
ABCDEFGHIJKLMNOPQRSTUVWXYZ
1234567890.,;:"&!?$

abcdefghijklmnopqrstuvwxyz   GILL SANS
ABCDEFGHIJKLMNOPQRSTUVWXYZ
1234567890.,;:"&!?$

When you are using serifs as a guide to type identification, it is important to remember that a typeface of a larger size or bolder weight is not always an exactly scaled reproduction of its smaller counterparts. Serifs that look attractive in small type, but not so pleasing in a larger size or bolder weight, are sometimes modified by the designer, who then creates a separate font of the bolder weight or one to be used in larger type sizes. If possible, always compare type in one size and weight to type of the same size and weight in the typeface book.

y y y **y y**   GLYPHA
y y y y   SLIMBACH

Serifs link one letter to the next, one word to the next. This type is easiest to read, especially in long copy.

While some sans serif faces may be more legible than some serif faces, they are not necessarily more readable. There are exceptions. Helvetica, as just one example, is sans serif. Its classic simplicity and perfect symmetry make this typeface as easy to read as many serif faces.

Modern typesetting programs can expand, condense, and curve type. Distortion can result. Depending on the resolution of the output device (or printer), the sharp edges of a typeface, such as finely chiseled serifs, may appear to be rounded. For positive identification, it is important to know what printing device has been used and at what resolution.

expanded and condensed type   UNIVERS EXTENDED,
UNIVERS, UNIVERS
CONDENSED

expanded and condensed type   UNIVERS ELECTRONICALLY
EXPANDED (120%) AND
CONDENSED (85%)

The x-Height

Another aid to type identification is studying the x-height. All lowercase letters have an x-height, and many of them have ascenders and descenders that can also help you distinguish one typeface from another.

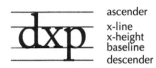 ascender
x-line
x-height
baseline
descender

The x-height is the height of the body of the typeface. The ascender is the part of the letter above the x-height. The descender is the part of the letter below the x-height.

LETTERS WITH ASCENDERS	b d f h i j k l t
LETTERS WITHOUT ASCENDERS OR DESCENDERS	a c e m n o r s u v w x z
LETTERS WITH DESCENDERS	g j p q y

The proportions of these elements vary among typefaces. The x-heights may be small or large; ascenders and descenders may be short or long.

d x p	ADOBE GARAMOND
d x p	CHELTENHAM
d x p	GOUDY OLD STYLE
d x p	NEW CALEDONIA

It is easy to confuse letters with similar shapes and characteristics, especially if you are not reading as slowly as you should. Let your eyes follow all contours of each letter as you read. Remember, the top half of letters is more recognizable than the lower half. Ascenders and descenders also help in quick letter recognition. Letters that have no ascenders or descenders are harder to recognize quickly.

PROOFREADING
Proofreading

Rhythm

A typeface design can also convey a certain rhythm. The more familiar you are with the typeface, the more pronounced the rhythm becomes. Study the shapes of each letter. Practice drawing them. Look at the whole body of type and try to feel its movement.

The five boxing wizards jump quickly.   AVANT GARDE GOTHIC

The five boxing wizards jump quickly.   EUROSTILE

The five boxing wizards jump quickly.   ITC BENGUIAT GOTHIC

The five boxing wizards jump quickly.   LUBALIN GRAPH

The five boxing wizards jump quickly.   POPPL-LAUDATIO

EIGHT

Understanding the Typesetter's Language

Instructions to typesetters, called type specifications (specs) or markup, are written in a technical but very simple language. They are, as proofreader's marks are, a universal shorthand code that everyone connected with typesetting and printing must know—and most certainly the proofreader, who must determine whether the instructions were followed.

In this age of computerized typesetting, the proofreader likely won't see a manuscript completely marked up as you would on advertising copy. Instead, you will see the art director or designer's specs on only a sample page or two. But it will be your responsibility to make sure that the specifications noted on those sample pages are treated correctly and consistently throughout the typeset copy.

There are three primary pieces of information that the typesetter must have:

- the type font
- the point size of the type and the leading (the distance, in points, from the baseline of one line of type to the baseline of the next line of type)
- copy depth, usually in picas; line length, in picas; and margins (flush left, flush right, flush center, or justified (flush left and right), in picas or inches)

These specifications are commonly written as a formula. For the following paragraph, the specs would be written as follows:

85

Bembo bf ital 11/14 [x18]

This paragraph is set in Bembo (the name of the typeface) bold (the weight) italic (the posture). The typeface size is 11 points, the leading is 14 points, the [is a flush left instruction, the] is a flush right instruction (therefore, the copy is justified), and x18 is an 18-pica line length. These specifications will be explained in the following pages.

There are secondary instructions to the typesetter, as well, and they are explained below.

TYPE FONT

A type font is a complete set of characters in one *typeface* and one *style*. It contains all uppercase and lowercase letters and includes punctuation marks, numerals, and other special characters. To make sure that the proper type font has been set, match it to the corresponding one in a typeface book.

Typeface

Typeface is the overall family design of the type, and it will be specified to the typesetter by its family name, which is often copyrighted. Helvetica, Times New Roman, Frutiger, and Goudy Old Style are examples of typeface names.

Style

The weight, width, and posture of a typeface are the style of the typeface. Each is independent of the other.

Weight is determined by the thickness of strokes. A typeface can have many weights: thin, extra light, light, book, medium, demibold, semibold, bold, extra bold, ultra bold, heavy, and black. Descriptive names and the degree of thickness can vary by typeface. A typeface book is the best guide to weight. The specified weight of the typeset copy should be an exact match to the corresponding weight in the book. You may also consult Web sites that sell fonts (search "buy fonts"), but it may be difficult to match weights between the computer screen and your typeset copy. When weight is not included in the type specifications, book or medium weight will be typeset.

HELVETICA LIGHT

Type set in lightface often fades into the background, making reading difficult.

HELVETICA MEDIUM

Type set in medium weight is easier to read. Especially in small sizes, medium weight is more distinct than light or bold weights.

HELVETICA BOLD

Boldface type is difficult to read, particularly in small sizes. The density eliminates some of the white space inside and around the characters.

All fonts have weight. Type of any size can be any weight. Small type can be bold or light or any weight in between. So can large type.

Width is the amount of horizontal space each character covers. A typeface can have many widths: extra condensed, condensed, compressed, book, elongated, extended, expanded, or wide. As with weights, specific names and degrees of width can vary with each typeface. When width is not included in the type specifications, book width will be typeset. The characters in this paragraph are set in book width, as is the first paragraph below.

UNIVERS

This typeface is set in book width. It is much easier to read than a typeface that is of condensed or expanded width.

UNIVERS CONDENSED

This typeface is condensed. As the characters are squeezed together, a single character could easily be overlooked.

UNIVERS EXTENDED

This expanded typeface should be proofread character by character. It is as difficult to read as large display type.

All typefaces have width. Type of any size can be any width. Small type can be expanded or compressed. So can large type.

Posture is the slant of the typeface. Display and script faces often have unique slants that are not labeled. Many text faces have fonts that slant to the right (italic or oblique). The upright posture of a text typeface is called roman. Don't confuse this with the Roman type classification. When posture is not included in the type specifications, roman posture will be typeset. The characters in this paragraph are set in roman posture.

Italic typefaces are harder to read than roman faces.

All typefaces have posture. Type of any size can have any posture. Type can even be backslanted.

The word *regular* has been omitted as a description of typeface weight, width, or posture. A common but ambiguous term, it is often used by those seeking a type style that looks most "normal." As different typefaces may look regular or normal in a variety of ways, a more precise specification is essential. What's more, neither typesetters nor proofreaders can be expected to do their job well with such vague instructions. Unless there actually exists a regular style for the particular typeface being set, those who typeset and proofread the type should ask for a more exact specification.

Size

The third characteristic of a typeface is probably its least understood dimension. It is important to remember that two different typefaces of the same point size may not look—or actually measure—the same in size. That is why comparing type against one of the same face and size in a typeface book is the most accurate way to measure.

Many typeface books do not contain all faces and sizes of type, however, which is why the point gauge is the most convenient and common method of measuring. But it's an inexact science and has become even more so with the advent of computerized typesetting and photographic equipment. Even to the observant and practiced eye, it is an approximate measure, and those proofreaders who insist on absolutes may not easily understand it.

POINTS AND PICAS

Typefaces and other typographical elements such as rules and bullets are measured in *points*, a system used by typesetters in the United States. Other units of measure exist in Europe and other parts of the world, one being the metric measure, which, until recently, has met with resistance in the United States.

Today's typesetting systems almost universally measure a typographic point as exactly $\frac{1}{72}$ of an inch.

Spaces created by type (leading, indents, line length, and copy depth) are measured in *picas*. Pica measurement is simply an extension of the point measure. As the measurement in the point system gets larger, the measuring unit changes from points to picas, just as when measurement in inches gets larger, the measuring unit changes from inches to feet.

There are 12 points to a pica, 6 picas to an inch. It is with this larger unit that space is measured.

To measure type size and space, the proofreader will need the same tool the designer and the typesetter use: a metal or transparent ruler (also called a line gauge) calibrated in points and picas. These measures are also available on a plastic sheet, often about 5 inches by 10 inches, called a transparency.

In today's typesetting systems, typefaces may be set in sizes from 1 point to 1000 points or larger, at increments of a tenth or even a thousandth of a point. Type measuring from 5 to 8 points is often seen in footnotes, ingredient labels, classified advertisements, and sometimes contracts. A magnifying glass for proofreading this *mouse type* is recommended.

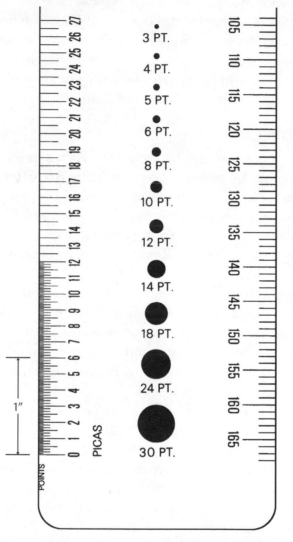

Gauge for measuring points and picas (*left*), size of bullets (*center*), and agate lines (*right*).

mouse type	mousetype
mouse type	mousetype
mouse type	mousetype
mouse type	mousetype

Type sizes that allow for more comfortable reading, such as the text in books, newspaper or magazine articles, and advertisements, are within the 9- to 14-point range, depending on the size characteristics of a particular typeface. Type this size is commonly referred to as *body type* or *text type*.

body type	body type	**body type**	body type
body type	body type	**body type**	body type
body type	body type	**body type**	body type

Larger type sizes, often called *display type*, range from 14 points upward. Type that is 72 points measures about 1 inch tall (from top of ascender to bottom of descender).

A type character is considered to occupy space on an imaginary block called the *body* of the type. For most typefaces, the ascenders and descenders fill—or at least come close to filling—the vertical space of the type body, and the point size of the type is nominally the height of the body. A 10-point body produces 10-point type, an 11-point body produces 11-point type, and so on.

Some typefaces may look larger or smaller, depending on the length of their ascenders and descenders and, especially, their x-heights. The face, not the actual measurement, conveys the visual impression of size. But it is the body that produces the actual type measurement.

The following lines are all set in 11-point type.

The five boxing wizards jump quickly.　　BODONI

The five boxing wizards jump quickly.　　ITC CENTURY

The five boxing wizards jump quickly.　　GILL SANS

The five boxing wizards jump quickly.　　GOUDY OLD STYLE

The five boxing wizards jump quickly.　　HELVETICA

USING THE POINT GAUGE

Even with a point gauge, type cannot be measured for accurate size, although the proofreader can get an approximate measurement. Ascenders and descenders of many typefaces (and the proofreader must be experienced enough to know which typefaces) *almost* fill the body of a block of type. Find a word that contains both an ascender and a descender. By placing the point gauge at its 0 mark at the tip of the ascender, then measuring to the bottom tip of the descender, an approximate size can be determined. A capital letter, if it is the height of the ascenders in that typeface, can be used instead of the ascender to measure.

Apple　　ITC CENTURY, 42 POINT

USING THE TRANSPARENCY

The plastic transparency shows points and other typesetting measurements, including one that measures a capital letter or, on some transparencies, a lowercase letter.

The letters on the transparency do not measure a true point size. They only measure a standard-size capital letter for standard-

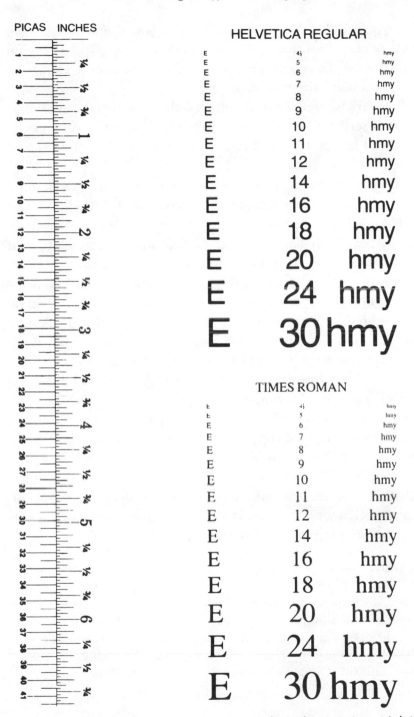

Gauge for measuring picas and inches (*left*) and point sizes (*right*).

size typefaces. For example, a 12E letter on the accompanying transparency illustration will closely match the height of a 12-point capital letter. Lowercase letters on the transparency are for measuring standard-size lowercase letters.

Some transparencies show letters with serifs; others have letters with no serifs. It is best to measure serif type on transparencies with serif letters, sans serif type on transparencies with sans serif letters.

When matching type against capital or lowercase letters on a transparency, the proofreader must know whether the particular typeface being measured is of average size or whether it is one of those typefaces that are designed smaller or larger than average. If the typeface is designed small, the letters on the transparency cannot be used to measure it. In this case, consult a typeface book for comparison. If you are unsure about the type design or the actual size, ask fellow workers who are more familiar with type. A little study and practice, and you will soon know as much as they do. If you have sample pages from the designer, you can directly compare the size of type on the typeset copy with the size of the corresponding type on the sample.

Lines, bullets, and other shapes of type, used to call attention to particular passages of copy, are not automatic measurements either. The size and weight of these elements are determined by the designer. Specifications are written as point measurements in the margin beside the copy where the lines or shapes are to appear. The proofreader will match these rules, bullets, stars, or squares to corresponding ones on the transparency.

A rule may be a ½-point hairline rule _____, a 1-point rule _____, a 2-point rule _____, and so on. The more points specified, the heavier and thicker the rule. Bullets, stars, and squares are also measured in points. They become larger as the point size increases (1-point bullet ·, 2-point bullet •, and so on). The most precise way to measure these shapes is with a transparent gauge that contains ruled lines, bullets, and stars in a variety of sizes.

Wrong Font

If any of the elements in a type font has been set wrong, it has been set in the wrong font.

Typeface	If Helvetica type was specified but the copy was set in Goudy, it is in the wrong font.
Weight	If Helvetica bold was specified but the copy was set in Helvetica light, it is in the wrong font.
Width	If Helvetica condensed was specified but the copy was set in Helvetica extended, it is in the wrong font.
Posture	If Helvetica italic was specified but the copy was set in Helvetica roman, it is in the wrong font.
Size	If 10-point Helvetica was specified but the copy was set in 12-point Helvetica, it is in the wrong font.

The proofreader may circle the mistake in the copy and use the marginal instruction, a circled **wf**. It would be more helpful to the typesetter, however, if you circled the mistake in the copy and wrote out the specific instructions, such as **set Goudy bold** or **set Goudy 10 pt** (circled). This keeps the typesetter from having to search back through the type specs for information on the correct font.

LEADING

The space around the type is equally important in design. It provides the frame for the type. If it is too tight, it can squeeze the type and make it dark and unreadable. If there is too much space, the type can float, disrupting the reading pattern.

Leading (rhymes with "sledding"), also called line spacing, is the second primary piece of information a typesetter must have to set type. This is the distance, measured in points, between the baseline of one line of type to that of the following line. This applies both in heads and in body copy.

Line Spacing

There is no rule dictating the proportion of leading to type size. It is a design decision, determined primarily by the typeface design, its size and style, its x-height, and the length of its ascenders and descenders.

1. This paragraph is set in 10-point type with no extra leading. It is written as **10/10**. The first 10 indicates the size of the type in points. The following 10 is the line height in points. When the line height is the same measure as the type size, it means that there is no extra leading, that the type is *set solid.* In most solid-type copy, the descenders on one line will almost touch the ascenders on the line below it. There will be exceptions in solid type where ascenders and descenders are not close to each other, or where they may even overlap (or bump), depending on the typeface design. This is a good reason always to measure the leading, even if you think you may know what it is just by looking at it.

2. This paragraph is set in 10-point type with 1 extra point of leading. It is written in the formula as **10/11**. The 10 indicates the size of type. The 11 is the line height.

3. This paragraph is set in 10-point type with 2 extra points of leading. It is written in the formula as **10/12**. The 10 indicates the size of type. The 12 is the line height.

HOW LEADING IS DETERMINED

Some typefaces have large x-heights or long ascenders and descenders that will naturally call for more space between lines for attractive layout and comfortable reading. When there is not enough space between the lines of type, an often unattractive "bumping" will occur, as a descender on one line hits an ascender on the next line. If you don't know whether this bumping was intended by the designer or accidental because of a miscalculation, you should circle the affected letters and write **bumps** (circled) in the margin.

These two lines of type illustrate "bumping" ascenders and descenders.

Typefaces with small x-heights or short ascenders and descenders need less space between the lines, sometimes even negative line spacing. This is a reduction of space between lines of type to less than the point size of the typeface. For example, 12-point type with a line height of 11.5 points has negative 0.5 points of line spacing. Negative line spacing is very common in heads and is also occasionally used in body type for special design reasons.

When upper- and lowercase letters are used with numerals (such as in a name and address), an uneven "color" is often created because of the size difference between the numerals and the lowercase letters. A more even distribution of space will occur by adding extra lead between the lines. The proofreader may offer this suggestion, but it will normally be a decision made by the designer.

The Colony Bank 9870 Third Avenue Central City, Idaho 60800	The Colony Bank 9870 Third Avenue Central City, Idaho 60800

Line length is another element of consideration for good leading. The longer the lines of type, the more space is needed between them to read smoothly and easily to the next line.

Additional leading is sometimes desired as a break between paragraphs. The instruction is not written in the standard formula shown at the beginning of the chapter. Instead, it is written in the margin beside the place in the copy where the extra leading is to appear. If the line height in a paragraph is 10 points, and an extra 4 points of leading is needed between paragraphs (making the line height 14 points between paragraphs), the designer will designate it by writing +4 between the paragraphs that need the extra space above. It normally will not be circled.

The leading between the example paragraphs 1 and 2 on page 96 has an additional 4 points of space. Compare the difference with the space between other paragraphs in this book.

USING THE POINT GAUGE

To determine if the leading is correct, measure the distance from the baseline of one line of type to the baseline of the next line. This should equal the leading specified by the designer. For example, to measure the leading in example paragraph 1 on page 96, place the 0 mark of the point gauge at the base of one line and follow the gauge down to the base of the line below. The measure should be 10 points. Therefore, the type is 10-point set solid (10/10). Type specifications of 10/11 (measure example paragraph 2 on page 96) would mean that the type size is 10 points with 11 points of leading. To measure the extra leading between example paragraphs 1 and 2, place the 0 mark of the point gauge at the base of the last line of paragraph 1. Follow the gauge down to the base of the first line of paragraph 2. It measures 14 points, meaning there are 4 extra points of leading between the two paragraphs.

USING THE TRANSPARENCY

Transparencies often contain another measuring gauge, a series of boxes with lines, by which leading can be determined. Use only the boxed lines for 10-point leading on your gauge. Go to example paragraph 1 on page 96. Place the top line of the box at the base of the first line of copy. The remaining 10-point lines should fall at the base of each of the lines that follow. If they don't, the leading is wrong.

1. This paragraph is set in 10-point type with no extra leading. It is written as **10/10**. The first 10 indicates the size of the type in points. The following 10 is the line height in points. When the line height is the same measure as the type size, it means that there is no extra leading, that the type is *set solid*. In most solid-type copy, the descenders on one line will almost touch the ascenders on the line below it. There will be exceptions in solid type where ascenders and descenders are not close to each other, or where they may even overlap (or bump), depending on the typeface design.

WRONG LEADING

If you are correcting a leading problem, you will mark the point of trouble, then in the margin write and circle one of the following: **add lead**, **delete lead**, **wrong lead**, or **equalize lead**.

The space between lines
one and two contains one
extra point of lead. The
lines below are set solid.

When it is not the entire line of type, but only a word or two that are improperly aligned, draw one horizontal line above the word (or words) and another line below. Make two horizontal lines in the margin, or write **align** (circled) in the margin. See Table 6.1 on page 56.

This sentence is improperly aligned.

Word Spacing

Spacing between *typewritten* words is set in mechanical spacing units. Each word is a uniform distance from the next. It cannot be adjusted in any way.

The space between *typeset* words is specified in a typesetting program to begin at a precise (but not mechanical) distance from each word. The amount of space that will fall between each word is calculated according to the characteristics of a particular typeface design and size. But unlike on copy prepared using a typewriter, spacing adjustments between words can be made by the typesetter. Even when the spacing problem affects just a few words, the typesetter can adjust the spacing to open the tight spots or close up space.

As there are no instruments for the proofreader to measure word spacing, you will be guided by the optical spacing effect. Between the affected words, use a *plus sign* to open space and a *verti-*

cal line to close space. Marginal instructions are the words **open** and **close**, respectively.

This is not a job for the beginning proofreader or for anyone else who is not accustomed to working with typeset copy. Ideally, you will receive guidance from an expert for a few weeks, and you will soon develop good judgment and a fine eye for spacing problems. It is your job to help the typesetter through these tight, and sometimes loose, spots.

IRREGULAR WORD SPACING

There is the possibility of irregular word spacing in all typeset copy, but most particularly in lines with very large or very small type or with all-capitalized type.

Where the spacing is too tight, words will run together.

If it is too far apart, the spaces create gaps that the eye must jump over to read.

Sometimes spacing problems will affect only a word or two in a sentence.

Copy with justified columns usually has word spacing irregularities from line to line. There is no easy solution. The copy is restricted to the narrow confines of equal-length lines. So that the copy will meet both margins exactly, word spacing most likely will be different despite special custom fitting by the typesetter.

When several consecutive lines of type are set with wide word spacing (to accommodate a justified margin), this can compound the spacing problem with "rivers" of white space that overpower the horizontal flow of type. One solution is to add extra words to fill in the gaps. Or, if allowed by the designer, you may break and hyphenate words.

Word breaks at the end of consecutive lines of justified type are still another problem and one that is often ignored, mainly because fixing a

word break on one line often causes a
new word break on the following line.
It may be that the style allows word
breaks in two—but no more—consecutive lines. If there are more than
two word breaks in a row, you should
circle them.

Some spacing adjustments can be made by the typesetter, but
unless the line length is increased or the copy is rewritten to the
exact measure of the line, there is no happy solution. Working
with justified copy is often the proofreader's (and the typesetter's)
most frustrating and difficult chore.

The proofreader should look for word spacing problems in all
typeset copy. Bad spacing is unattractive, is hard to read, and can
destroy an otherwise artistic and creative endeavor.

Letterspacing

Letterspacing varies according to the size and design of the typeface and is formatted, automatically or manually, in a typesetting
program. But spacing problems between characters can and do
occur. The proofreader judges good letterspacing not with the
printer's tools but by how it looks on paper. As with word spacing,
it is an optical measurement, not a mathematical one. Each character, and the space surrounding it, then the entire word or line of
words, must be judged. It requires careful observation and practiced judgment to spot when one character is too close to or too
far from the next one.

READING
HELVETICA, 42 POINT,
MECHANICALLY SPACED

READING
HELVETICA, 42 POINT,
OPTICALLY SPACED

BAD LETTERSPACING

The most likely candidates for irregular letterspacing problems are lines with very small or large type or with all-capitalized type.

An unfortunate choice of typeface can also create an insurmountable problem with certain combinations of characters:

LAWYER   TIMES NEW ROMAN

The only solutions are to change the wording or the typeface, or to change the word from upper- to lowercase type.

Sometimes, though, type is intentionally set far apart or close together. *Positive* spacing is often used to set apart all-capital letters and words. *Negative* spacing, where characters touch, even overlap, can also be deliberate. Both are used as attention-getting devices, primarily in advertising. As both are hard to read, they normally are not used in long copy.

ACADEMIC   GOUDY OLD STYLE

Locomotion   LUBALIN GRAPH

If the designer wants unusual spacing between characters, it must be expressed precisely to the typesetter. Regular spacing (the default in the typesetting program) does not require special instructions. To correct tight or wide spacing between characters, the proofreader uses the same marks and instructions as for word spacing.

Em and En Spaces

PARAGRAPH INDENTS

The blank spaces used at the beginning of a paragraph are called *em* or *en spaces*. The em, so called because the capital letter *M* in most typefaces is as wide as it is high, is a square of space as wide (and as high) as the size of type being set. In modern typesetting, it is considered only a horizontal space.

This paragraph has a 1-em indent. A 1-em indent on 10-point type is a space that is 10 points wide. A 1-em indent on a line containing 6-point type is a space that is 6 points wide. A 1-em indent is most often used for copy with short lines. Long lines of copy require more. It is a design decision.

Sometimes a designer will specify indents in picas instead of ems. The proofreader should make sure that the designer intended picas, especially if the indent seems wider than it would normally be. Don't confuse the em and the pica when measuring.

An *en space* is one-half the width of an em, measuring about as wide as the lowercase letter n. A 1-en paragraph indent on 10-point type is 5 points wide. This paragraph has a 1-en indent.

DASHES

Dashes (short, ruled lines) are also measured in ems and ens.

There are four kinds of dashes that must be measured: the en dash, the em dash, the 2-em dash, and the 3-em dash. In most typefaces, an em dash is the length of the type size in points. An en dash is half the length of an em dash. A 2-em dash is twice the length of an em dash, and a 3-em dash is three times as long. The length of a hyphen, which is also a dash, is determined by the typeface design and size.

On typewritten copy, the hyphen and en dash are indicated by one horizontal line between characters or words (-). The em dash is indicated by two typed horizontal lines (--). This should be circled, and a precise measurement should be given to the typesetter. As there is no typewritten symbol that can indicate a 2-em dash or a 3-em dash, horizontal lines are also used for each. The designer must circle the lines and specify the size dash in the margin. If space allows, the size of the dash is sometimes written directly in the text.

Hyphens A hyphen is used to divide a word at the end of a line. Other uses of the hyphen are to express a unit, such as with simple compound adjectives, nouns, or numbers; as suspension in a series; with some prefixes; and to avoid ambiguity:

> chocolate-covered nut
> decision-maker
> twenty-three
> 2- and 3-hour sessions
> ex-employee
> re-sign the contract

Hyphens are typically designed to be centered on the x-height. And when used with lowercase letters, the position is usually ideal. When a hyphen is used with capital letters, it sometimes appears too low. Watch for this and ask the typesetter to raise it to an optically centered position. (Parentheses and brackets are also designed for lowercase letters and should sometimes be raised to line up with capital letters.)

En Dash   The en dash is used to express a range of numbers, such as page numbers, years, and references:

> pp. 551–558
> during the period 1860–1865
> chapters 1–3

The en dash should not be used to designate "from ... to" or "between ... and"—for example, "from noon–midnight" or "between June–August."

Use an en dash between compound adjectives and to separate hyphenated groups of words:

> pre–Space Age technology
> high-temperature–low-temperature averages

Em Dash   The em dash marks a sudden break in thought or tone; sets off (for clarity or emphasis) an added explanation or parenthetical element; separates an introductory series and the main part of the sentence; and introduces a name after a quotation:

> I was scared—but who wouldn't have been?
>
> The gloves—the hat, too—were leather.
>
> The book, the pen, the paper—all were on my desk.
>
> ". . . and a touch of grammar for picturesqueness."
> —Mark Twain

2-Em Dash   A 2-em dash substitutes for missing letters in a word.

> Robert J—— is the culprit.

3-Em Dash   A 3-em dash indicates a missing word.

> I went to Lake —— to sail my boat.

A 3-em dash is also used in bibliographies when the author of a work is the same as the author of the work that immediately precedes it.

> Ogilvy, David. *Confessions of an Advertising Man,* New York: Atheneum, 1963.
> ——. *Ogilvy On Advertising,* New York: Crown Publishers, Inc., 1983.

Always watch for incorrect usage of these dashes.

COPY DEPTH, LINE LENGTH, MARGINS

Copy depth, line length, and margins are the final instructions to the typesetter. Line length and margins—but not copy depth—are part of the formula.

Copy Depth

Copy depth refers only to the body copy depth on a page and does not include heads or page numbers. Copy depth is the distance, in picas, from the first line through the last, including leading and any other spacing that may have been specified. A vertical measurement may be given to the typesetter. If used, it will be written beside the formula like this: **22 picas deep**. Or the depth may only be implied if a layout accompanies the type. The proofreader must check copy depth accordingly. For example, the copy depth of this page is 41 picas 10 points.

The exact space in which the copy will fit is determined before the type is set, by a procedure called copyfitting. Using a simple mathematical formula, the designer calculates the area required for a given amount of typed copy in a specified typeface and size. If copyfitting is not done beforehand, the outcome may not be a happy one. Miscalculation can cause the copy to run short of the planned copy depth. Or it could run too long. And either can ruin a creative concept.

Even when copyfitting has been calculated, a rough layout (but with exact measurements) often accompanies the typed copy to the typesetter. This layout may (or may not) give the typesetter an alternative to overcome spacing problems, if there are any. If there is a mutual understanding between the designer and the typesetter, copy that runs too short may be set ½ point larger, or if it runs too long, it may be set ½ point smaller to fit the space in the layout. But most designers do not rely on this haphazard method of fitting copy to space.

Line Length

The way to measure the horizontal length of the lines of typeset copy will depend on the margins. As all lines in justified copy measure the same (except the last line of a paragraph), the line length is the number of picas it takes to fill any one line. With a rag margin, where the line beginnings or endings vary in horizontal position, the longest line should be measured. This line cannot exceed the specified line length, although some of the other lines will be shorter.

The pica measure for line length on the copy specifications formula is always preceded by an **x**. Instructions for a 14-pica line length will be written **x14**.

There are several design considerations that determine the line length: typeface design, type size, leading, the amount of copy to be typeset, and the amount of space the designer has to work with. Generally, the larger the size of type, the longer the line. A normal line of typeset copy has between 55 and 70 characters, or 9 to 12 words.

Lines that are exceedingly long or short are hardest to read. When a line of type is too long, the eyes tire before reaching the end. In addition, the eyes must then jump a longer distance back to the beginning of the following line. Short lines interrupt sentence structure. They also create more word breaks. When the eyes must continuously jump from one short line down to the next short line, it causes reader fatigue.

Margins

Column margins are the vertical patterns created by the lines of type. Instructions must be given for both the right and left margins. Following is a variety of margins from which the designer selects.

FLUSH LEFT

All lines begin at the same horizontal position on the left margin, except paragraph indents, if indicated. If none is indicated, the first line of each paragraph is also flush left. Copy spec marks in the formula are written either with a circled **fl** or a [(left bracket).

FLUSH RIGHT

All lines end at the same horizontal position on the right margin. Spec marks in the formula are written with either a circled **fr** or a] (right bracket).

RAGGED LEFT OR RIGHT

The left or right margin has no specified minimum stopping point, although there is always a maximum stopping point, or line length. The typesetter ends the line where it looks appropriate within that specified line length, usually alternating a short line, then a longer line, followed by a shorter line, making a smooth, rhythmic pattern. (See "Margin Rag" on page 110.) A ragged margin usually ensures even word spacing. Spec marks are written with **rl** or **rr** (circled) or a **wavy vertical line**.

Each column of type has two margins. So where there is a flush or rag left margin, obviously there must be a flush or rag right margin. And instructions for both must be specified. This paragraph is set flush left/rag right.

Each column of type has two margins. So where there is a flush or rag left margin, obviously there must be a flush or rag right margin. And instructions for both must be specified. This paragraph is set rag left/flush right.

JUSTIFIED

With justified copy, both margins line up horizontally except where paragraph indents are indicated. If none is indicated, the first line of each paragraph is also flush left, creating the need for extra leading between paragraphs as a break. Spec marks for justified copy are written **fl/fr** (rarely used) or with the circled word **justify** or [ ] (two brackets). The text in this book has justified margins.

As mentioned in "Word Spacing" on page 99, the amount of space between the words, and characters, may be different from line to line because the lines must be of the same length. The proofreader should watch for very obviously irregular letterspacing or word spacing. Sometimes it can be corrected; other times it cannot without adding or cutting copy. Word breaks also occur more often in justified copy than in copy with a rag margin.

CENTERED

Each line of copy is centered on the column or page. None is aligned horizontally on either column edge. Spec marks are the circled word **center** or] [(two brackets facing out).

Centered copy allows for even spacing between
characters and words, as there are no restrictions except
the maximum line length. One shortcoming, however,
is that the uneven edges make reading more difficult,
which is why centered copy is generally used only
for short copy such as heads, advertisements, or invitations.
The lines of this paragraph are centered.

It is best to center lines optically rather than mechanically. Optical centering on lines of type that have quotation marks at the beginning and at the end is especially recommended.

ASYMMETRICAL

When there is no predictable pattern for line endings, the copy is either typed on a page exactly as it should appear typeset line for line, or is typed in a regular manner but interrupted by a hand-drawn Z at the exact place where each typeset line should break. The formula instruction in the margin is **LL** (meaning set line for line).

Example: This line]is marked for[asymmetrical breaking.

This line
is marked for
asymmetrical breaking.

WRAPAROUND

What an inexperienced proofreader might initially judge as a bad rag or "hole" could simply be a wraparound margin. Pay close attention to copy specs and to the designer's layout. A wraparound is used to follow the outline of a photograph or illustration. Spec marks are the words **wraparound** or **wrap** or **runaround** (circled), accompanied by specific dimensions and a precise spacing layout.

The proofreader should pay close attention to the rag created by the wraparound, as an unattractive marginal rag, space gaps, and too many word breaks can result if the designer did not copyfit before the type was set. Most designers will at least furnish the typesetter (and the proofreader) dimensions in picas of the space where type is not to be set. An alternative to precise pica measurement of each line in the wraparound is an outline or drawing of the copy block, including the pattern and dimensions of the wraparound area. If the wraparound does not fit as smoothly as the designer wants, often the writer will change a word here or there for a nicer fit.

MARGIN RAG

The rag is the pattern created by the line endings on all unjustified margins. While there is no consensus on what a good rag should look like, there are some accepted guidelines that the proofreader should follow, unless instructed otherwise.

The main function of type is to be read. A good, marginal rag in the body copy contributes to a smoother read. And although heads and subheads usually break after a thought or for sense, visual appeal of the rag is also a consideration.

A good rag evokes rhythm. It does not call attention to itself. It weaves in and out, its lines alternately short and long, but not varying in length by more than 2 ems. A good rag avoids a sharply defined pattern. It avoids consecutive lines that are the same length and give the impression of justified copy. A good rag also avoids word breaks on consecutive lines, if possible.

Bad rag

It is the rare body of typeset copy that has an
ideal rag throughout with no manual intervention.
The rag depends on the combined efforts
of the designer, an experienced typesetter, and a knowledgeable
proofreader, and a whole array of other
factors (the typeface, the line length, the amount of
space allocated for the copy). A good
typesetter can often adjust bad margin rags, but conscientious
designers do not leave it all to chance. For unless each character
has been counted (by copyfitting) so that the words
will fall exactly where the designer envisions, there could be
some disappointments. Even after careful planning,
it may be necessary to move copy or adjust spacing to achieve
the best results. Good rags take time and planning.

Better rag

It is the rare body of typeset copy that has an ideal rag
throughout with no manual intervention. The rag depends
on the combined efforts of the designer, an experienced
typesetter, and a knowledgeable proofreader, and a whole
array of other factors (the typeface, the line length, the
amount of space allocated for the copy). A good typesetter
can often adjust bad margin rags, but conscientious
designers do not leave it all to chance. For unless each
character has been counted (by copyfitting) so that
the words will fall exactly where the designer envisions,
there could be some disappointments. Even after careful
planning, it may be necessary to move copy or adjust
spacing to achieve the best results. Good rags take time
and planning.

Whatever your preference in rag pattern, you will be guided by the designer's instructions. Some may specify a rag with no word breaks, which guarantees an irregular rag. There may be wide gaps of white space on the ragged margin edge.

Others may specify a rag that looks almost justified. And, as it does in justified copy, this will create irregular letterspacing and word spacing and increase the chances of abrupt line endings. Word breaks at line endings also will occur more often. Sometimes spacing and word breaks can be adjusted by the typesetter with the aid of proofreader instructions. But spacing and word-break problems may often be unavoidable unless the actual copy is changed line by line.

Rags that create fewer spacing problems and word breaks are centered copy rags or rags in copy set flush left/rag right. The hardest to correct are rags in copy that resemble justified and those in copy set rag left/flush right.

WORD BREAKS

There is some basic agreement on the subject of word breaks among those who work with type:

- Avoid incorrect word divisions.
- Avoid word breaks at the end of three or more consecutive lines of type unless the columns are narrow.
- Avoid word breaks at the end of the first line of a page or column.
- Avoid word breaks at the end of the last line of a page or column.
- Avoid two-letter word breaks or short word breaks.
- Avoid breaks on an already hyphenated word or before a dash.
- Avoid proper noun breaks.

The rule that is always observed (except sometimes in newspaper copy) is the first one. Incorrect word breaks must never be allowed. And many other breaks can be avoided, such as two-letter breaks at the end of a line that could be broken at the next syllable. This often solves a bad margin rag, as well. While there are some basic guides to word division, remember that there are exceptions to almost every rule. Even dictionaries can disagree on syllables. Before marking your correction, consult a dictionary.

The other rules should be followed when possible. The proofreader should question all undesirable breaks, even if you see no solution. The writer or designer may want to avoid the bad break as much as you do and may rewrite or reposition that part of the copy. On the other hand, necessity may sometimes dictate a deviation from the rules (except incorrect word divisions) if the copy cannot be changed to avoid a bad break or if the break makes a better marginal rag.

The in-text mark for a bad word break is to circle the word, then write out the entire word, in syllables, in the margin. Or separate the word at the correct break with a Z mark inside the copy.

PRINTER'S PROOF

Once the final version of text is completed, electronic files are delivered to the printer. At first, only a few copies are made. These printer's proofs, also called press proofs, bluelines, brownlines, laser proofs, or digital proofs, are sent to the customer for inspection. Although not of the same quality as the final print will be, the proof is an accepted interpretation of how the finished product will appear.

Usually one who is an expert in print production will read the proof for density, color, imperfections in the printing plate, among many other things. The proofreader may be asked to check it to make sure all the elements are in place and pages are in order (see the checklist for printer's proof in Appendix C). As this proof is only a sample copy made from a negative or plate, no extraordinary measures should be taken to protect it. Use an indelible-ink pen to mark errors or blemishes in the copy.

The Proofreader's Tools

Two 6-inch nontransparent rulers
Magnifying glass
Fine-line, indelible-ink red pen
Lead pencil (colored)
Pica and point gauges
Dictionary
Grammar/punctuation handbook
Word usage reference
Stylebook and/or style sheet
Key to proofreader's marks
World atlas
Foreign language dictionaries, as required
Trade names reference
Thesaurus or synonym finder
Typeface guide
Graphic arts handbook

McGraw-Hill's General Instructions for Freelance Proofreaders

HOUSE STYLE

Use *The Chicago Manual of Style* (*CMS*), fifteenth edition, *Merriam-Webster's Collegiate Dictionary*, eleventh edition, and our general house style sheet. The style sheet takes precedence over *CMS* and *Webster's* when there is a conflict.

You should always receive a terms/names list and sometimes copy editor's notes and clean-up notes. Read the notes over before you begin to proofread and refer to them as needed. Highlighted are any instructions pertinent to your work.

MARKING GALLEY PAGES

Contrary to *The Chicago Manual of Style* instructions, draw guidelines from the text to corrections in the margin. Use standard proofreading symbols and make sure your corrections are readable. We prefer that you use red pencil; don't use green, because that is our typesetters' color. If you are reading after another proofreader, use a different color pencil. Sign your name on the first page of galleys in the pencil you chose.

Mark typesetting errors, which include bad breaks, with a circled PE in the margin next to the correction. Look up bad breaks in *Webster's* (not *CMS*), and write the correct breaks in the margin and a circled "per Web" next to the correction. Do not put a circled BB in the margin. If there is reflow from first pages to second, or revised, pages, and bad breaks occur in the reflowed copy, those also are to be marked PE. Anything you mark to be changed that is *not* a PE, mark EA (editor's alteration) and circle in the margin. Note that McGraw-Hill allows end-of-line breaks from recto to verso pages and vice versa.

Do not mark broken type or dirt spots. It's just the photocopier.

Point out obvious loose lines and mark those PE as well.

Point out orphans (and mark as PEs only those that are a result of a hyphenated word on the previous line). Our definition of an orphan is ANYTHING shorter than the paragraph indent as well as a partial word; i.e., the only word on the last line of a paragraph cannot be part of a hyphenated word (unless it is a compound word). (For example, it is okay to have "far-reaching" break at the hyphen so that "reaching" is alone on the last line of the paragraph. But it is *not* okay to have "rebroadcast" break so that "broadcast" is alone on the last line.) Except for "un-," a line should never end with fewer than three characters, and a line should always begin with a syllable of at least three characters. Note that our typesetting program (Quark) will break contractions and they shouldn't be broken—please mark.

Do not mark *widows* unless you are reading revised galley pages.

When deleting words before a punctuation mark, use the close-up sign to show that the punctuation should remain.

Do not circle anything in the text unless you mean "spell out." Circle, in the margin, anything that should not be set, including queries and proofreading symbols. Do *not* circle corrections that should be set.

QUERIES

We do not expect you to copyedit the book; your primary task is to find PEs, especially if you are proofreading first galleys against the manuscript, and to correct spelling or grammar errors. If, in your silent read, you find consistency or sense problems or if you have suggestions for additions, deletions, reorganizations, or other editing, write your query or suggestion in the margin or on a Post-it® note.

Do not query misspelled words. First, check the terms list and notes to see if the word was intentionally treated in a certain way. If not, look it up in *Webster's* and correct it. Also, be careful when you are correcting hyphenation. Some words are hyphenated differently depending on whether they are used as verbs, adjectives, or nouns.

If you notice a consistent "error," please call the editorial services manager before you "correct" or query it throughout the galleys.

STAGES OF PROOFREADING

Proofreading first galley pages Proofread galleys against the copyedited manuscript. Mark PEs, which may include bad breaks, loose lines, and orphans as defined above, and EAs.

If a large portion of copy has been omitted (more than you can write clearly in the margin), attach the manuscript page(s) to the galley on which the copy should be inserted. Indicate the missing copy on the manuscript page, and indicate on the galley where that missing copy should go.

Double-check cross-references to other chapters or sections of the book. Make sure the chapter number is correct and the chapter title is exactly as it appears elsewhere in the book. If there is any information to be filled in later, draw a guideline from the place where the missing information will appear to the margin and write "to come," *and circle.*

Check spelling of names, places, etc., against the names list. If this step interferes with your proofreading, make a separate pass through the galleys to check them.

Carry over art and/or photo keying. Transfer from the manuscript to the galley page any unresolved queries.

If you are dry reading, look for spelling and grammar errors as well as sense and consistency. When you find errors during the dry read, check against the manuscript to see if they are actually overlooked PEs. Also check against the terms/names lists and notes in case there are instructions or explanations for the errors you find.

Look for and point out orphans and, in seconds or revised galley pages, widows as well.

Proofreading second or third galley pages Make sure corrections marked on the first galleys have been made on the second galleys and that no new errors have been introduced.

Mark PEs, which include bad breaks, loose lines, widows, and orphans as defined previously, and EAs.

Dry read as described above.

Reading final pages Read as if you are a consumer, correct spelling and grammar errors, and query as needed. Point out widows and orphans. (We define a widow as the first line at the top of a page whose width is less than three-quarters of the full measure.)

A page must start with at least the last two lines in a paragraph; it must end with at least the first two lines of a paragraph. If necessary, the latter rule can be broken before the first rule. If the first rule must be broken, there must be no widow as the first line of a page.

Proofreading Checklists

Typed Copy

FIRST READING

Read the instructions.

Compare with original text—deviations from text, doubly typed words, typographical errors, and incorrect word breaks.

SECOND READING

Begin compiling your style sheet.

Read for content—fact or format inconsistency, word usage, sentence structure, subject and verb agreement, repetition of thoughts or phrases, and incorrect math.

Check the language mechanics—capitalization, punctuation, spelling, grammar, and hyphenations; legal mandates, footnotes, bibliographies, table of contents, index, tables, and charts.

THIRD READING

Read for completeness and perfect copy.

Compare with your style sheet notes.

If the copy has been retyped, it should be read again by the proofreader.

Typeset Copy (First Galleys)

FIRST READING

Compare with dead copy (never with the designer's layout)— deviations from text, doubly typed words, typographical errors, incorrect word breaks, pairs of quote marks and parentheses.

SECOND READING

Follow the type specifications—check typeface and font (weight, width, posture, and size), leading, line length, paragraph indents, copy depth, column margins (rags), alignment (vertical and horizontal), and centering.

THIRD READING

Look at size and placement of rules, dashes, hyphens, and bullets; widows and orphans; page sequence; page and line breaks; letterspacing and word spacing; consecutive word breaks; dirty copy or broken characters (if applicable); and type density.

FOURTH READING

A final read for completeness of copy, including heads, subheads, captions, legal information, and footnotes.

When marking typeset copy, remember to mark a circled **PE** (printer's error) or **EA** (editor's alteration) beside each correction or change. Printer's errors will be corrected at no charge, but the editor's alterations will be charged to your company.

After corrections have been made by the typesetter, read the entire copy again. If there is no time to read it all, at least re-read a line or two above and below the line where the correction was made (as well as the corrected line, of course). Watch for new word breaks, line breaks, and page breaks. Double-check the table of contents to make sure it is consistent with the newly corrected copy. Indexing should also be checked again by the editor or proofreader.

If the copy has been re-typeset, it should be read again by the proofreader.

Revised Galleys

FIRST READING

Compare with dead copy—final check for typographical errors and deviations from first galleys; inclusion of all copy elements, including heads, subheads, captions, footnotes, tables, lists, legends, logos, photographs, legal information, trademarks, and copyright line.

SECOND READING

Review type specifications and designer's instructions to the type-setter; check for uniform positioning and alignment of all elements (numbers, heads, subheads, and captions); watch for un-even, crowded, or loose spacing; check for correct pagination, and compare copy against table of contents.

THIRD READING

Look for overall completeness.

Printer's Proof

It is always a safeguard to read the printer's proof against the final text, although this is usually impossible for book-length projects. The proofreader should review the proof, watching for the following: inconsistent leading and alignment, positioning of elements, missing elements, spacing, type density, and dirty places or broken characters on the proof. If changes are needed, they should be marked with a circled **PE** or **EA**.

Published Works

It is the masochistic proofreader who reads again at this stage. Finding an error too late only adds to the anxiety of an already nerve-wracking occupation. When the proofreader sees the article or advertisement in final print, the page should be quickly turned. If there is an error, it will undoubtedly be caught and reported to you by someone whose own errors you correct daily. Don't go looking for trouble.

Words and Phrases Commonly Confused or Misused

a ~ an

ability ~ capability ~ capacity

accept ~ except

ad ~ add

adapt ~ adept ~ adopt

admission ~ admittance

adverse ~ averse

advert ~ avert

advice ~ advise

affect ~ effect

aid ~ aide

all ready ~ already

all together ~ altogether

alley ~ ally

allude ~ elude

allusion ~ delusion ~ illusion

altar ~ alter

ambiguous ~ ambivalent

amend ~ emend

among ~ between

amoral ~ immoral

amuse ~ bemuse

and ~ plus

anecdote ~ antidote

ante- ~ anti-

appraise ~ apprise

assassin ~ murderer

assay ~ essay

assume ~ presume

assure ~ ensure ~ insure

attorney ~ lawyer

audience ~ congregation ~ spectators

avenge ~ revenge

avoid ~ evade

baited ~ bated

bare ~ bear

bazaar ~ bizarre

because ~ since

beside ~ besides

better than ~ more than

between ~ among

blatant ~ flagrant

bloc ~ block

boat ~ ship

born ~ borne

bough ~ bow

brake ~ break

breach ~ breech

breadth ~ breath ~
  breathe

bring ~ take

burglary ~ robbery

calendar ~ calender

cannon ~ canon

canvas ~ canvass

capital ~ capitol

censer ~ censor

ceremonial ~ ceremonious

cession ~ session

chafe ~ chaff

childish ~ childlike

chord ~ cord

cite ~ sight ~ site

classic ~ classical

climactic ~ climatic

clench ~ clinch

common ~ mutual

compare to ~ compare with

complementary ~
  complimentary

compose ~ comprise

comprehensible ~
  comprehensive

confute ~ refute

connote ~ denote

consul ~ council ~ counsel

contemptible ~ contemptuous

continual ~ continuous

convince ~ persuade

corps ~ corpse

could care less ~ couldn't
  care less

cove ~ lagoon

credible ~ creditable ~
  credulous

criteria ~ criterion

dairy ~ diary

delusion ~ illusion

deprecate ~ depreciate

desert ~ dessert

diagnosis ~ prognosis

different from ~ different
  than

discomfit ~ discomfort

discreet ~ discrete

disinterested ~ uninterested

dispute ~ refute

distinct ~ distinctive

dual ~ duel

e.g. ~ i.e.

effective ~ effectual

egoism ~ egotism

elegy ~ eulogy

elicit ~ illicit

emigrate ~ immigrate

eminent ~ immanent ~
  imminent

energize ~ enervate

enthused ~ enthusiastic

entitled ~ titled

equable ~ equitable

ever so often ~ every so often

explicit ~ implicit

farther ~ further

faze ~ phase

fewer ~ less
flail ~ flay
flair ~ flare
flaunt ~ flout
flounder ~ founder
forceful ~ forcible
foreword ~ forward
fortuitous ~ fortunate
gamble ~ gambol
got ~ gotten
grisly ~ grizzly
hangar ~ hanger
hanged ~ hung
hardly ~ scarcely
hardy ~ hearty
he/she/I ~ him/her/me
historic ~ historical
hyper- ~ hypo-
I/you ~ myself/yourself
i.e. ~ e.g.
idle ~ idol
if I was ~ if I were
imply ~ infer
in ~ into
in behalf of ~ on behalf of
incidence ~ incident
incite ~ insight
incredible ~ incredulous
indict ~ indite
ingenious ~ ingenuous
intense ~ intensive
inter- ~ intra-
irregardless ~ regardless
its ~ it's
judicial ~ judicious

lay ~ lie
lead ~ led
leave ~ let
lend ~ loan
lesser ~ lessor
lighted ~ lit
lightening ~ lightning
like ~ such as
loath ~ loathe
loose ~ lose
luxuriant ~ luxurious
masterful ~ masterly
material ~ materiel
mean ~ median
medal ~ meddle ~ metal
militate ~ mitigate
miner ~ minor
moral ~ morale
nauseated ~ nauseous
naval ~ navel
noisome ~ noisy
official ~ officious
or ~ nor ~ neither
oral ~ verbal
ordinance ~ ordnance
orient ~ orientate
palate ~ palette ~ pallet
passed ~ past
peace ~ piece
peaceable ~ peaceful
pedal ~ peddle ~ petal
periodic ~ periodical
perquisite ~ prerequisite
persecute ~ prosecute
perspective ~ prospective

pertaining ~ pertinent
plain ~ plane
practicable ~ practical
practically ~ virtually
pre- ~ pro-
precede ~ proceed
premier ~ premiere
prescribe ~ proscribe
pretense ~ pretext
principal ~ principle
prophecy ~ prophesy
prostate ~ prostrate
proved ~ proven
quiet ~ quite
regard ~ regards
regardless ~ irregardless
respectfully ~ respectively
raise ~ rise
role ~ roll
sanitarium ~ sanitorium
scraggly ~ scraggy ~ spindly
seasonable ~ seasonal
select ~ selected
sensual ~ sensuous
set ~ sit

shear ~ sheer
stationary ~ stationery
than ~ then
that ~ which
their ~ there ~ they're
these kinds ~ this kind
to ~ too ~ two
tortuous ~ torturous
transient ~ transitory
trooper ~ trouper
try and ~ try to
turbid ~ turgid
unexceptionable ~
    unexceptional
usage ~ use
use to ~ used to
vain ~ vane ~ vein
valuable ~ valued
venal ~ venial
weather ~ whether
when ~ where
which ~ that
who ~ whom
who's ~ whose
you're ~ your

General Office Style Sheet

This style sheet is for a fictitious consulting firm, whose clients are city and county governments.

FORMAT

- Unless otherwise noted, format assumes vertical spacing of six lines per inch.
- Examples of the following are attached to the sheet.

Letters

Elements and Spacing Between Elements

Heading or letterhead
  (3 blank lines)
Date
  (3 blank lines)
Address
  (2 blank lines)
Reference lines
  (2 blank lines)
Salutation
  (1 blank line)
Body
  (1 blank line)
Complimentary close
  (4 blank lines)
Signature
  (2 blank lines)
Stenographic references
  (1 blank line)
Enclosures

Notes

- All lines are set flush with the left margin.
- Paragraphs are not indented.
- There is one blank line between paragraphs.

Long Letters

Left/right margins	1″/1″
Tabs	0.5″
Top margins	1st page, 1.5″; 2nd page, 1″
Bottom margin	1″
Paper	Standard engraved letterhead

Note

- On letters longer than one page, type "Page _____ of _____" one-half inch (three lines) from the bottom of the page.

Short Letters

Left/right margins	1″/1″
Tabs	0.5″
Top/bottom margins	Centered vertically on page
Paper	Standard engraved letterhead

Envelopes (Standard Engraved #10)

Left margin	3.5″
Top margin	2″

Notes

- When an address line must be continued on a second line, indent the second line two spaces.
- Suite, room, or apartment numbers follow the street address on the same line.

Reports to Clients

Elements and Style

Left/right margins	1.5″ on edge to be bound; 1″ on other edge
Title page	Position to match cutout in report cover
Table of contents	Top/bottom margins—1st page, 1.5″; subsequent pages, 1″
List of figures	Top/bottom margins—1st page, 1.5″; subsequent pages, 1″

Chapter title page	Top/bottom margins—1.5"/1"
All other pages	Top/bottom margins—1"/1"
Paragraphs	Indent 0.5", no space between paragraphs
Page numbering	Style—table of contents through list of figures, lowercase Roman numerals; body of report, continuous Arabic numerals
	Location—center of page, 1/2" from bottom
	If printing both sides of page, insert blank pages if necessary to start each chapter on an odd-numbered page.
Endnotes	Superscripted Arabic numerals
Paper	20# "client" bond

Memos

Left/right margins	1"/1"
Tabs	0.5"
Top margins	1st page, 1.5"; 2nd page, 1"
Bottom margin	1"
Paper	1st page—preprinted memo form; 2nd page—standard bond

TYPE STYLE

HP LaserJet 3380

Reports to clients	Times New Roman 12 pt (PS)
Memos	Courier (10 CPI)
Long letters	Times New Roman 12 pt (PS)
Short letters	Times New Roman 12 pt (PS)
Envelopes	Times New Roman 12 pt (PS)

GENERAL STYLE ELEMENTS

Dates

- June 1, 2005
- June 2005
- Summer 2004

Numerals

- Spell *one* through *nine*; numerals from *10* on.
- *3%,* not *three %* or *three percent.*
- *99%,* not *ninety-nine %* or *ninety-nine percent.*

Punctuation

- Put titles of speeches in quotes.
- Italicize names of books and newspapers.
- Put chapter titles and article titles in quotes.

CAPITALIZATION, HYPHENATION, ITALICS, POSSESSIVES, PUNCTUATION, AND SPELLING

(adj)	adjective	(pl)	plural
(cn)	collective noun	(poss)	possessive
(dict)	dictionary	(sing)	singular
(n)	noun	(v)	verb
(pa)	predicate adj		

A

B

Brzezinski, Wertmüller, and Velázquez, Engineers

C

the city (other than client's city)
the City (client's city)
City of Chicago
the county (other than client's county)
the County (client's county)
cul-de-sacs (pl)

D

database (n, adj)
DeKalb County
Department of Community Affairs (DCA)
Department of Housing and Urban Development (HUD)
Department of Natural Resources (DNR)
drafting film (do not use trade name)

E

F

Federal government
fee-simple (adj)

G

H

House Bill 215

I

IL (Illinois, in addresses)
Ill. 34 (Illinois State Highway 34)

J

K

L

the Legislature (client's state)

M

the Midwest
multi-family (adj)

N

O

P

Ph.D.'s (pl)

Q

R

Robinson and Associates

S

Senate Bill 14
the Soil Erosion Control Act

T

tax-exempt (adj)
townhouse (n, adj)

UV

WXYZ

the Zoning Ordinance (client's ordinance)

MISCELLANEOUS

Manuscript Style Sheet

The following manuscript is the source for the style sheet beginning on p. 135.

America Discovers Its Wilderness

Until the early 20th century, wilderness survived only as a byproduct of the movement to reserve public lands for other purposes. Then the Forest Service began experimenting in the early 1920's.

Arthur Carhart, the agency's first landscape architect, helped preserve the Trappers' Lake Region of Colorado from development, and Aldo Leopold, in 1924, created the Gila Wilderness in New Mexico, the first official wilderness area in the United States.

Wilderness Inventory

Chief Forester William Greeley ordered inventories of all undeveloped National Forest lands larger than 230,400 acres in 1926. Soon after, rules were established for managing "primitive areas." By the mid-1930's the agency had designated nearly 14 million acres of primitive land.

The leading advocate of wilderness preservation in the 1930's was Bob Marshall, who in 1937 became head of Recreation and Lands for the Forest Service. In 1939 Chief Forester Ferdinand Silcox approved Marshall's plan to inventory, study,

and reclassify primitive lands as wilderness areas to provide
them greater protection. . . .

Wild and Scenic Rivers Act

Congress passed the Wild and Scenic Rivers Act in 1968
to preserve portions of 50 rivers on Federal land in their
free-flowing state. Many additions to this system followed.

The Wilderness Act transferred 9 million acres of National
Forest wilderness land into the wilderness system and required
review of the 5 million acres of remaining primitive land for
possible inclusion. Beyond the scope of the Wilderness Act were
millions of acres of undesignated but undeveloped land in the
National Forests that were also potential wildernesses. . . .

Eastern Wilderness Areas

Almost all the eastern National Forests had been created from
cut-over and partially roaded land and, although many of the
forests had grown back, none of them were as pristine as the
forests of the West. The Forest Service wanted to create a
separate "Wild Areas" System in the 1970's for eastern areas,
arguing that the Wilderness Act did not allow inclusion of
cut-over areas. . . .*

---

*Dennis Roth. "America Discovers Its Wilderness," Our American Land. U.S.
Government Printing Office: 1987, pp. 77–79.

STYLE SHEET: AMERICA DISCOVERS ITS WILDERNESS		
CAPITALIZATION **HYPHENATION** **ITALICS** **POSSESSIVES** **PUNCTUATION** **SPELLING** (adj) adjective (cn) collective noun (dict) dictionary (n) noun (pa) predicate adj (pl) plural (poss) possessive (sing) singular (v) verb	**A** agency	**B** byproduct
C Arthur Carhart Chief Forester Congress cut-over (adj)	**D** *Dates* 20th century mid-1930's	**E** East eastern Eastern Wilderness Act (so-called)
F Federal Forest Service	**G** Gila Wilderness William Greeley	**H**

I	J	K

L	M	N

Aldo Leopold	Bob Marshall
	Midwest
	Multiple Use-
	   Sustained Yield
	   Act of 1960
		Numbers
		all-numerical style
		14 million
		National Forest(s)
		Northeast

O	P	Q

R	S	T
reclassify/ reclassification Recreation and Lands roaded (adj)	Ferdinand Silcox South Summer	Trapper's Lake Region

U-V	W	X-Y-Z
	West Wild and Scenic Rivers Act (1968) "Wild Areas" System Wilderness Act the Wilderness Society (the Society)	

MISCELLANEOUS FACTS/NOTES

STYLE

initial-caps head, boldface, centered
initial-caps subhead (lowercase articles, prepositions, conjunctions),
    book weight, italic, flush left
flush left first paragraph under subhead, indent following paragraphs
    1 em
comma before *and* in series
line endings—no word breaks
Adobe Caslon typeface, 11/16 x24. +5 before subs

Client Style Sheet

The corporate structure and titles for the Peoples and Southeast Corporation are given below. The style sheet begins on p. 140.

THE PEOPLES AND SOUTHEAST CORPORATION
The "Corporation"
Subsidiaries of the Corporation
(Note: Indent indicates subsidiary status.)

PEOPLES AND SOUTHEAST GEORGIA CORPORATION

The Peoples and Southeast National Bank
　Peoples and Southeast Capital Corporation
　Peoples and Southeast Securities Corporation
　The Onondaga Corporation
　P&S Real Estate Services, Inc.
　　Peoples and Southeast International Bank
　　　Peoples and Southeast International Bank of New Orleans
Peoples and Southeast Mortgage Corporation
PSGA Funding Corporation
P&S Business Credit, Inc.
P&S Capital Corporation

PEOPLES AND SOUTHEAST TRUST COMPANY, INC.

Peoples and Southeast Trust Company (Georgia), N.A.
Peoples and Southeast Trust Company (South Carolina), N.A.
Peoples and Southeast Trust Company (Florida), N.A.

PEOPLES AND SOUTHEAST INSURANCE SERVICES, INC.

P&S FAMILY CREDIT, INC.

P&S Family Credit of Alabama, Inc.

P&S Family Credit of Florida, Inc.

PEOPLES AND SOUTHEAST FLORIDA CORPORATION

The Peoples and Southeast National Bank of Florida

Southeast Land Sales, Inc.

Southwest Land Sales, Inc.

PEOPLES AND SOUTHERN CORPORATION

The Peoples and Southern National Bank of South Carolina

Carolina Atlantic, Inc.

P&S Financial Services, Inc.

Peoples and Southern Systems, Inc.

Peoples and Southern Realty Corporation

STYLE SHEET FOR
THE PEOPLES AND SOUTHEAST CORPORATION

USAGE/PLACEMENT

- Registration mark on a P&S service (such as MasterCard®)—once per page.
- P&S logo in box must have registration mark.
- Member(s) FDIC—must be used in ads that mention deposit services; must be used on all TV ads; Seniors Club; do not use on Trust ads.
- Equal Housing Lender logo—use on any ad that mentions real estate or mortgage loans.
- Plural for acronyms is with apostrophe (IRA's, ATM's).

TYPEFACE

- Caledonia—copy
- Caslon 540—heads

LEGAL FOR ALL PRINT

- ©2006 The Peoples and Southeast Corporation (except Peoples and Southeast Insurance Services, Inc.)
- P&S® logo (all print)

TRADEMARK RULES

- Always use as an adjective, modifying a generic or common name for the services. (Money Saver® banking services).
- Do not use as a general descriptive adjective.
- Never use as a verb.
- Never use as a noun. Never: Open a Money Saver® today.
  Use: Open a Money Saver® account today.
- Do not use in possessive form, such as P&S's.
- Do not pluralize a service mark.
- Do not couple service marks.
- In textual material, provide service marks with distinctive appearance by using all capital letters, italics, quotation marks, or different color or type size.
- Use proper notice for registered marks by placing a ® next to the mark.

CAPITALIZATION, HYPHENATION, ITALICS, POSSESSIVES, PUNCTUATION, AND SPELLING

(adj)	adjective	(pl)	plural
(cn)	collective noun	(poss)	possessive
(dict)	dictionary	(sing)	singular
(n)	noun	(v)	verb
(pa)	predicate adjective		

A

account officer

American Express® Travelers Cheque™

annuity

Answer Center

asset-based

Atlantic Southeast Airlines

Automated Cash Management

Automated Teller Machines

automated teller network

B

Bank 'N Shop Centers

Bank-by-Computer

Bank-by-Phone

BankCard Center

benefits package

benefits plan

Better Business Banking services

Big Saver Account

Bonus Checking account

Branch Manager

buy outs

C

cardholder

Cash Management Officer

Cash Management Services

cashier's checks

Certificates of Deposit (CD)

Certified Employee Benefit Specialists

Check Safekeeping

CIRRUS®

closely held (adj)

Commercial Premium Investment Account

Common Stock Fund

Corporate Cash Management

Custom wallet checks

Customer Service Representative

D

data bases
disability insurance

E

energy-efficient (adj)
energy-saving (adj)

F

Family Credit Services

fax

Federal Deposit Insurance Corporation (FDIC)

Federal Income Tax Form

financial specialist

fixed rate

Fixed Term (IRA)

Flat Fee Checking

401(k)

full-cost

full-service (adj)

G

Gold Coast (Florida)

Gold Reserve

Government Banking Division

Government Banking Services

H

HONOR^{SM}

I

Income Fund

Individual Market Investment Account

Instant Banker(s)** (see Misc. Facts/Notes)

Instant Banker transaction

Instant Banking—Do not use as a noun

Instant Banking Card

Instant Checking

Instant Money Loan

InstantCheck Debit Card

Insurance Services

interest bearing (adj)

interest checking account

Investment Advisors

IRA* (see Misc. Facts/Notes)

J

K

KEOGH's (pl)

L

Loan pack
lock box

M

Market Investment Account

Market Investment Account
Instant Check (NOT Accounts)

Market Line account

Market Reviews

Master Trust

Master Trust Department

Master Trust services

Master Trustee

MasterCard®

MasterCard® gold card

MIA/IRA

Minimum Balance Checking

money market (n, adj)***

Money Saver® account***

Money Saver® Checking***

mutual funds

N

Newcomer Guide

Newcomer Services

no-obligation (adj)

NOW Checking (no ®)

O

Operations Group

P

P&S Answer Center

P&S Bank's (poss) (but not P&S's)

P&S Executor/Personal Representative

P&S Family Credit

P&S Market Reviews

P&S Trust and Financial Officer

The Peoples Bank of Tallahassee

Personal Banker

Personal Identification Number

Personal Trust Officer

policyholders

Preferred MasterCard®

Premium Investment Account

Public Finance Division

Q

R

Relationship Manager

Ready Equity Account (home equity loan)

Ready Reserve

Regular Business Checking

regular checking

resell

Revolving Account™ (one line)

R-values (n)

S

safe deposit boxes**** (see Misc. Facts/Notes)

self-directed (adj)

Self-Directed (IRA)

seniors account

Seniors Club

setup

Southeast, South

T

TARTAN Plus™ (see Misc. Facts/Notes)

Tax Anticipation Notes (TAN's)

tax-deferred (adj)

Tax-Deferred Annuities

tax-exempt

Tax-Exempt Lease

Telephone Banking System or Telephone Banking

term insurance

Time Deposit Account(s)

Travel Checking account

Travel Dollars

traveler's cheques or traveler's checks

travel-size bank

trust officer (or P&S Trust Officer)

T-shirt (n)

U

universal life

U.S. Treasury bill rate

V

Variable Rate (IRA)

VISA®

VISA® gold card

W

WIZARD℠ banking machines

X

Y

Your money's worth®

Z

MISCELLANEOUS FACTS/NOTES

- 175 branches all over GA; more than 290 Automated Teller Machines
- 160 branches throughout FL
- 387 branches throughout Southeast (387 employing over 11,353 people)
- 111 years of service (1894–2006)
- The P&S Answer Center—1-800-555-5555
- 239-RATE
- Seniors Club (55 and older)
- TARTAN Plus is a registered trademark of Recognition Equipment, Inc.
- *IRA—Fixed rate only. Substantial penalties may apply to early withdrawals from time deposit IRA's.
- **Instant Banker—AVAIL®/CIRRUS® charges apply to use on non–P&S automated teller machines, however.
- ***money market, Money Saver—Under license of agreements, these marks may not be used outside of designated Southeastern states.
- ****Safe deposit boxes—where available

PEOPLES AND SOUTHEAST SECURITIES LOCATIONS

Atlanta

1. Suite 1501
   78 North Avenue, N.E.
   Atlanta, Georgia 30346
   Local: (404) 555-1212
   Toll Free: 1-800-555-5552

2. 1 Perimeter Center West, N.W.
   Atlanta, Georgia 30346
   Local: (404) 555-2121
   Toll Free: 1-800-555-5553

Augusta

3. P&S National Bank Building
   523 Grant Street
   Augusta, Georgia 30902
   Local: (404) 555-1221
   Toll Free: 1-800-555-5554

Knoxville

4. First Tennessee Building
   Suite 1301
   16 South Helton Street
   Knoxville, Tennessee 37902
   Local: (615) 555-1212 Knoxville
           (615) 555-2121 Maryville
           (615) 555-2211 Oak Ridge
   Toll Free: 1-800-555-5555

Tampa

5. Eastshore Center
   Suite 16
   715 North Eastshore Boulevard
   Tampa, Florida 33607
   Local: (813) 555-1211
   Toll Free: 1-800-555-5556

Ft. Myers

6. Suite 201
   14 Second Street
   Ft. Myers, Florida 33901
   (located in First Atlantic Bank of Ft. Myers)
   Local: (813) 555-2212
   Toll Free: 1-800-555-5557

Ft. Lauderdale

7. One Financial Plaza
   18th Floor
   Ft. Lauderdale, Florida 33394
   Local: (305) 555-1112
   Toll Free: 1-800-555-5558

Florida Corporate

8. The Peoples and Southeast National Bank of Florida
   Eastshore Center
   715 North Eastshore Boulevard
   Tampa, Florida 33607
   Toll Free: 1-800-555-5559

Glossary

alignment, horizontal the positioning of lines of type so that the ends of lines meet at the same horizontal point. The type may be flush left, flush right, or justified.

alignment, vertical the positioning of type on a line so that the base of each character rests on a common baseline; also called base alignment.

art all artwork and photographs; also all original copy to be reproduced.

ascender the part of lowercase letters that extends above the x-height. The letters *b, d, f, h, i, j, k, l,* and *t* have ascenders.

author's alteration (AA) author's change to copy.

back slant style of type that slants backward (opposite of italic).

bad break (BB) incorrectly hyphenated word at the end of a typed or typeset line; also, a divided word at the end of the last line of a column or page.

bad copy any copy that is illegible to the typesetter.

baseline an imaginary line where all characters rest. Descenders extend below the baseline.

bleed excess area required on art to extend the printed image beyond the trimmed edge(s) of a page.

blueline (brownline) a preliminary printer's proof for inspection purposes.

body type text type used for reading, not display.

boldface (bf) typeface weight that is heavier (bolder) than normal.

book type body or text type; used for the text or main body of a printed piece.

border decorative line(s) surrounding a block of type or art.

broken rule a broken line; also called leaders.

broken type type that has not reproduced distinctly and looks broken in one or more places.

brownline see *blueline*.

bullet a dot of any size used to itemize or for ornamental purposes.

cap height height of a capital letter from its base to the top of the letter.

caps (uppercase) capital letters of the alphabet.

caps and lowercase (initial caps, clc, ulc) type style in which the first letter of a word is capitalized, with the remaining letters lowercase, or the first letter of every word is capitalized, the remaining letters lowercase.

caps and small caps (csc) type style in which two sizes of capital letters are used in a word or words. The small caps are usually about two-thirds the height of capital letters.

caption (cutline) identifying or explanatory text that accompanies an illustration or photograph.

centered type style in which a line or lines of type are set centered on a column or page.

characters per pica (CPP) the average number of type characters that will fit in the width of one pica.

column rule rule used to separate columns of type.

comparison reading comparing two pieces of copy to make sure they are identical.

condensed type style in which the characters are narrower than the normal design of the typeface.

copy manuscript before it is printed; also all typewritten material, photos, and illustrations before they are printed.

copyfitting a mathematical procedure to determine the typeface and size and style of type that will enable a given amount of copy to fit in a given area.

copyholder one who reads dead copy aloud to the proofreader.

crop marks (register marks) crosses or other marks used to position photographs or copy.

cursive style of type that resembles handwriting.

cut to eliminate.

cutline see *caption.*

dead copy the original manuscript; a proofread, typed version of the manuscript; galleys used to compare against the most recent typeset version.

density the degree of darkness of type or a photographic or other image.

descender the part of lowercase letters that extends below the baseline. The letters *g, j, p, q,* and *y* have descenders.

display type larger, bolder, or more decorative type than that usually used in body text; primarily used in heads.

do not set (DNS) instruction to the typesetter not to set a word or words included in the copy.

dry reading see *noncomparison reading.*

edit to check a manuscript for facts, word usage, spelling, grammar, punctuation, and consistency of style and make changes thereto. The proofreader may be required to perform some editing functions.

editor's alteration (EA) editor's change to copy.

em a space that is the width, in points, of a given type size; used to measure indents and dashes.

en a space that is one-half the width of an em; used to measure indents and dashes.

extended (expanded) type style in which the characters are wider than the normal design of the typeface.

face see *typeface.*

family a group of fonts that are all variations of one basic design. The usual components of a type family are roman, italic, bold roman, and bold italic. These can also vary in width (condensed or extended) and in weight (light or thin to extra bold or black). Some type families have many variations.

flush left/flush right copy that is set to align horizontally at the left or the right. When margins are both flush left and flush right, the type is called justified.

flush paragraph   a paragraph with no indents.

font   a complete set of characters in a single style of a typeface; usually contains all of the upper- and lowercase letters, as well as punctuation marks, numerals, ligatures, and other characters.

footnote   note appearing at the bottom of a page, referring to a point in the text above.

format   the style, size, and overall appearance of a printed piece.

gauge (line gauge, pica rule)   a metal or plastic ruler calibrated in picas on one edge and inches on the other and used to measure type. Transparent rulers may also be calibrated in points.

gothic   black letter type resembling hand-drawn letters of scribes; also, sans serif type (in the United States).

gradation   range of tones in art, negatives, and reproductions.

greek   disarranged or jumbled type sometimes used in a proposed layout for the purpose of counting characters or judging type appearance.

gutter   margin (white space) where two pages meet at the binding; also, white space between columns of type.

hairline   a rule (line) usually measuring between 0.25 and 0.5 points thick; also, a thin stroke in serif type.

halftone   a photograph or other art formed by dots of varying size when a negative is created.

hanging bullets   type arrangement in which all bullets are set flush left and all lines of copy that follow them are indented.

hanging indent   paragraph structure in which the second and succeeding lines are indented on the left.

hanging punctuation   type arrangement in which hyphens, periods, and other punctuation marks at the beginning or end of a line of type are moved just outside the margin; used for aesthetic purposes; used primarily in justified copy.

hard copy   see *proof*.

head (headline)   title of an article or advertisement.

head margin   white space above the first line on a page.

indent (indention)   white space(s) at the beginning of a typeset line.

indicia identifying marks or indications.

inferior see *subscript*.

initial caps type style in which the first letter of every word is capitalized.

italic type style that slants to the right.

justified type copy in which each line of type is set to exactly the same length.

kern to adjust the space between characters; usually means to tighten.

kill to delete unwanted copy.

lead (leading, line space, line height) amount of vertical space, in points, between the base of one line and the base of the following line. A setting in which the leading is the same as the point size of the type is called solid type.

lead-in first few words in a block of copy set in a contrasting typeface.

leaders rows of dashes (rules) or dots (bullets) used to guide the eye across the page; used primarily in tables.

leading see *lead*.

legal lines mandatory copy such as trademarks, service marks, and copyright notices.

letterspacing spacing between individual characters.

ligature (lig) a character of type, such as *fi* and *fl*, combining two or more letters.

lightface (lf) typeface weight that is lighter than normal.

line art drawing(s) in black and white, with no gray tones.

line for line (LL, L/L) instruction to the typesetter to set line breaks exactly as they appear on the manuscript.

line gauge see *gauge*.

line height see *lead*.

line length maximum line length of copy, in picas.

line space see *lead*.

link the stroke connecting the top and bottom of a lowercase *g*.

live copy latest version of a typescript or typeset copy.

logo (logotype) the name, symbol, or trademark of a company.

loop the lower portion of a lowercase *g*.

lowercase (lc) type style in which letters or words are not capitalized.

margin area around type and illustrations that contains no printed elements.

mark up to mark type specifications on original copy.

measure length of a line to be typeset, in picas.

minus (negative) letterspacing/minus (negative) word spacing reduction in the normal space used between characters or words.

negative a photographic image in which color values are reversed; see also *minus (negative) letterspacing/minus (negative) word spacing*.

noncomparison (dry, silent) reading proofreading in which a single piece of copy is proofread without copy to compare it with.

nonreproducing type of pen or pencil whose impressions are invisible when copy is duplicated or printed; usually light blue.

offset a method of printing in which an image on a plate is transferred to a rubber cylinder and then to paper.

orphan the first line of a paragraph when it appears as the last line of a column or page; also, the last line of a paragraph when it appears as the first line of a column or page.

out, see copy (OSC) instruction to the typesetter that some of the original copy has not been typeset.

outline type style in which only a line appears on the outside edge of characters.

pic photograph.

pica unit of measurement for length and depth of copy. There are 6 picas in 1 inch and 12 points in 1 pica.

pica rule see *gauge*.

point unit of measurement for type size, leading, paragraph indents, dashes, and spaces. There are 12 points in 1 pica and 72 points in 1 inch.

point gauge a tool for measuring points. See also *gauge*.

positive letterspacing/positive word spacing increase in the normal space used between characters or words.

posture slant of a typeface.

printer anyone working in the printing trade, including typesetters/typographers.

printer's error (PE) error made by a typesetter or printer in production; there is no charge to the client for a PE.

printout see *proof.*

proof (hard copy, printout) sample sheet of printed material that is checked and corrected against the original manuscript. See also *reader's proof.*

proofreader person who reads typed or typeset copy against the original manuscript to make sure it is correct.

proofreader's marks shorthand symbols used to indicate alterations or corrections in copy. The symbols are standard throughout the communications and printing industries.

query question concerning copy by the proofreader to the writer, editor, designer, typesetter, or printer.

rag the side margins of typeset copy that is not set flush.

ragged type copy with an uneven margin on the left, right, or both left and right.

reader's proof sample sheet of typeset material for proofreading, on which corrections are made.

register marks see *crop marks.*

roman (Roman) style of type in which the upright strokes are vertical (as distinguished from italic, where the strokes are slanted); also, style of type with serifs.

rule line used for a number of typographic effects, including boxes, borders, and underscoring.

run to print.

run in to set type with no paragraph break or to insert new copy without creating a new paragraph.

runaround see *wraparound.*

running head a book, section, or chapter title repeated at the top of every page.

sans serif style of type with no serifs.

script style of type that resembles handwriting or writing with a brush.

serif a projection across the end of a stroke of a character; a style of type with serifs.

service mark a name, symbol, or other device identifying a service officially registered by and legally restricted to the use of the owner.

shoulder curved stroke of the *h, m,* and *n.*

sic (cq, ok) marginal note to the reader or typesetter that an unusual word, which might ordinarily be queried, is an approved spelling.

silent reading see *noncomparison reading.*

size the measure of a type character or characters in points.

solid type lines of type whose leading equals the point size of the type.

specs see *type specifications.*

spine curved stroke of an *s* or *S.*

stet proofreader's mark that indicates the copy marked for correction should stand as it was before the correction was marked.

straight copy type not accompanied by display elements such as photographs or drawings.

stress thickening of a curved stroke of a character.

stylebook (style sheet) an organized list of style points to which the manuscript must conform.

subscript (inferior) a small character positioned below and to the side of another character.

superior see *superscript.*

superscript (superior) a small character positioned above and to the side of another character.

swash decorative flourish on the serif of some characters.

terminal the end of a stroke not terminated with a serif.

text type type used in body copy, usually measuring from 9 to 14 points in size.

to come (TK) indication to the typesetter or printer that some copy is missing from the original text and will be forthcoming.

trademark a name, symbol, or other device identifying a product that is officially registered by and legally restricted to the use of the owner.

transposition (tr) common typographical error in which characters or words are not in correct order.

type generally, text or body type.

type specifications (pr specs) instructions to the typesetter or printer indicating how copy should be treated typographically.

typeface a full range of type of the same design family.

typesetter person who sets type.

typographical error (typo) typed or typeset error.

uppercase type style in which letters or words are all capitalized.

weight boldness of a font, based on the thickness of its characters' strokes.

white space any space that contains no printed element.

widow last line of a paragraph that is undesirably short.

width amount of horizontal space that a character covers.

word break breaking a word at the end of one line and continuing the word on the following line.

word spacing spacing between individual words.

wraparound (runaround) margins of typeset copy designed to fit around a photograph or illustration.

wrong font (wf) error in which a character is set in a typeface, style, or size other than that specified.

x proofreader's mark used to indicate dirty or smudged copy or broken type.

x-height the height of the main body of lowercase characters, excluding ascenders and descenders.

x-line the line that marks the tops of lowercase characters, excluding ascenders.

Index

The entry "Proofreader's marks" contains a comprehensive list of these marks. Typefaces are entered under their individual names.